FAILED GRADE

Copyright © Albert H. Soloway, 2006. All rights reserved. No part of this book other than Figure 11-1 may be reproduced or transmitted in any form or by any means, electronic or mechanical, including photocopying, recording, or by any information storage and retrieval system, without permission in writing from the publisher.

Published by
American University & Colleges Press™
An imprint of American Book Publishing
P.O. Box 65624
Salt Lake City, UT 84165
http://www.american-book.com
Printed in the United States of America on acid-free paper.

Failed Grade: The Corporatization and Decline of Higher Education in America

Designed by Lewis Agrell, design@american-book.com

Publisher's Note: This publication is designed to provide accurate and authoritative information in regard to the subject matter covered. It is sold or distributed with the understanding that the publisher and author is not engaged in rendering legal, accounting, or other professional service. If legal advice or other expert assistance is required, the services of a competent professional person in a consultation capacity should be sought.

Library of Congress Cataloging-in-Publication Data

Soloway, Albert H.
  Failed grade : the corporatization and decline of higher education in America / by Albert H. Soloway.
    p. cm.
  Includes bibliographical references and index.
  ISBN 1-58982-236-6 (alk. paper)
  1. Universities and colleges--United States--Administration.
  2. Education, Higher--United States--Administration.   I. Title.
LB2341.S59 2006
378.10973--dc22

2006000984

Special Sales

These books are available at special discounts for bulk purchases. Special editions, including personalized covers, excerpts of existing books, and corporate imprints, can be created in large quantities for special needs. For more information e-mail
info@american-book.com

FAILED GRADE

The Corporatization and Decline of Higher Education in America

By

Albert H. Soloway, Ph.D.

Dedication

Dedicated to my mother and father, Mollie Raphaelson Soloway and Bernard Soloway, Russian-Jewish immigrants to the United States who valued this country and the opportunities to gain an education and instilled that love of both in me.

Foreword

None of us with careers in teaching remembers a time when there was not a crisis in public education in America. The enormous expansion of schools and colleges in the last century has been followed by frustrating and continuous retrenchment. State economies are pinched, tuitions rise, levies fail, student achievement is problematic, and the prospects for solutions are few. Maybe this is simply a trait of public education in a democracy. When de Tocqueville wrote, education was in a rudimentary state in the nation, and he didn't speculate much about its future except by implication in his potent principle of the tyranny of the majority. And certainly we haven't defined and debated the issues, as they deserve.

A case in point especially in public education, as Dr. Soloway's book demonstrates, is the issue of governance, structure, in essence the purpose of universities. Over the past three or so decades the old collegial system of organization, shared governance in colleges and universities, has

Failed Grade

been largely replaced by a corporate structure of administration and purpose. The traditional, consultative system of shared governance, which valued advice and consent, discussion, academic freedom, a sense of the whole (the UNI- in the UNIVERSITY), has or is being replaced or subsumed by corporate "top-down" structures.

The consequences of this shift in values have been profound for universities and strangely, largely undiscussed, much less debated. Dr. Soloway examines critical issues of how the new financial imperatives and other corporate features have affected the whole university, faculty and administration, students, sports, degrees, the steady encroachment of money as the only value, the bottom line of education. One hopes, as he urges, that we should be more than casually concerned in this shift in values, about what has been lost. What has been gained? How, for instance, would the corporate university respond to serious threats to its academic freedom, like McCarthyism or worse? What has happened to institutional memory?

As a part of his examination of corporate-collegial issues, Dr. Soloway has brought many of his personal experiences as an academic administrator to bear. Of interest in themselves as well as the principles they help illustrate, together they form a kind of practical guide to aspects of academic administration. Not all will agree with the advice offered, but no one will doubt its candor and good intention. This is institutional memory put to good use.

It was my good fortune to have helped attract Dr. Soloway to our university. A man of high integrity and

Foreword

goodwill, he cared deeply for his college and the whole university. That care continues in this provocative critique and defense of collegial values.

Albert J. Kuhn, Professor of English Emeritus and former Provost (1971-79), The Ohio State University

Preface

This book began more than twenty years ago. I wondered why the quality of leadership I observed both in academia and industry was mediocre much of the time. I was reminded of the remark of Artur Schnabel, the twentieth century Austrian pianist and composer, that "mediocre is a high grade: there are very few above it and many below it." I thought perhaps my experiences were unique, but when I questioned friends and associates in other venues, it became apparent their experiences were similar to mine. The question was why? Obviously, people responsible for selecting senior leaders would want effective individuals whose organization would be better served because of them. Perhaps, the attributes of leadership were not well developed and that failure contributed to a flawed selection process. That was my initial thesis as I began to write this book.

I became more aware of the problems as I assumed leadership roles at two major universities and observed

Failed Grade

peers at my level and those in superior positions. The selection process for leadership positions was largely driven by self-promoters who knew how "to play the game" in relationships with those in superior positions or on selection committees. They were largely focused on themselves and controlling their own environments. Many had little concern with treating subordinates and others as they would wish to be treated, if the roles were reversed. Improving their organization and its environment did not seem a pressing priority.

While considering these ideas, I noticed a troubling development in higher education that was becoming more pronounced. Colleges and universities, always bureaucratic, seemed now much more motivated by business principles and the creation of a corporate culture (or as I call it, "corporatization"). On the surface, people might consider that development desirable. Corporations purportedly are concerned with increased efficiency to maximize profits. Is that such a bad objective for colleges and universities?

But universities, however, with the exception of online institutions, are generally not-for-profit. Educating students is extremely labor intensive, and should be. Quality time devoted by faculty to individual students can be highly beneficial in orienting and motivating them, helping them to focus on career goals and objectives, and maximizing their education. But that's not cost-effective. It is cheaper to use graduate students and staff. But are they as effective?

When institutions began the transition from a collegial environment to a corporate structure, there was no national discussion regarding the benefits and disadvantages of this change. Late as it is in the process, I hope this book will

Preface

promote serious discussion among administrators, faculty, and boards of trustees at universities where these changes have occurred. My experiences have not been at smaller, liberal arts institutions; therefore, I am unable to comment about the environment there.

My primary reason for writing this book is my commitment to the next generation of students, faculty and administrators to preserve an environment where educational quality is not eroded and holds the same value as mine did for me. Colleges and universities have been the crown jewels of American society, acting as a beacon to young people not only in the United States, but also around the world. Higher education is viewed as the entry point into the American job market and society. And those foreign students, who may return to their own countries, know that after obtaining a degree from an American university, others will respect them for their knowledge and competence.

This book is written for all who care deeply about higher education. It should interest members of boards of trustees with responsibility for an institution and those on state boards of higher education, as well as college and university presidents and chancellors, provosts, deans and chairs of departments, faculty, senior staff, students, and their parents. Since higher education has a significant impact on our future workforce and economy, every political entity, including federal and local government, must be concerned with the effectiveness of the learning atmosphere and academic expectations of students in colleges and universities. Among the issues, I examine the environment affecting higher education today, including

Failed Grade

faculty, administrators, and student attitudes; the evolving corporate culture and institutional governance; the importance of entrepreneurship and; the crisis in exploding tuition costs; and personal attributes of the successful academic leader.

What qualifies me to discuss the issues affecting higher education today? Of my forty-seven years of full-time employment in industry, research institutes, and academia, thirty-two have been spent in universities. First, I was a faculty member, then chair of a department before becoming dean of a college at two separate institutions. I returned to the faculty before retiring as dean and professor emeritus.

I hope this book will raise questions for those creating policy for higher education as well as provide suggested solutions for alleviating some existing problems. It's my belief that degrees, titles, and even knowledge are considerably less important than the learning experiences and environment and the rigor imposed on students by faculty members. The overriding purpose for colleges and universities is to educate the next generation, and everything else, however worthwhile, should be peripheral to that mission. As a society, we are indebted to the teacher in the classroom, laboratory, clinic, and art and performance studios for what we are ultimately able to achieve in our lives. Along with the education we receive from our parents, the standards that teachers set and the knowledge and experiences they impart will be with us throughout our lifetimes. And the real gift, as my father pointed out to me, is that education once imparted cannot be taken away.

Table of Contents

The Not-So-Recent Past 1
The New Financial Imperative 13
The Organization 33
Boards of Trustees 47
Boards of Regents or State Boards of Higher Education .. 57
Faculty and Tenure Matters 69
Students and Their Expectations 79
Education versus Indoctrination. How Social and Political
    Agendas Discourage Independent Thinking 93
The Problem with the Leadership-Selection Process 105
Attributes for Administrative Success and Failure 117
First Days on the Job 127
Administrative Sensitivity 135
Ethics and the Administrator 139
Recruitment, Retention, and Termination of Colleagues and
    Subordinates 149
Environment Creation, Decision Making, and Problem
    Solving 167

Failed Grade

Maximizing the Contributions of Associates.................. 179
Administrative Compensation, Financial Decision Making,
    and Budget Utilization 187
Colleges and Universities as Money-Generating
    Machines 199
The Ballooning Costs of Higher Education and Who's
    Worrying About It... 199
The Legacy of Faculty and Academic Administrators ... 223
The Murky Future of Higher Education in the United
    States 229
Endnotes... 257

Chapter One
The Not-So-Recent Past

Environment Prior to World War II

To understand the challenges facing higher education today, it's important to look back, since past conditions have created some of today's problems. Prior to World War II, enrolling in a higher education program was not considered a necessity. Many students viewed receiving a high school diploma as the end of their formal educational experience. Men entered the workforce, if jobs were available, or became apprentices in the trades. Women either stayed home or obtained secretarial positions until they married. Obviously, there were exceptions. Men who were interested in engineering, the sciences, law, and various health professions—and it was largely men—entered college to obtain the necessary education. Women who wanted to teach in elementary and high schools—largely the only profession open to women at the time except nursing— entered so-called "normal" schools or

Failed Grade

teacher-training colleges where they received the appropriate preparation. Most women continued to teach only until they were married, since married women were expected to stay home and raise a family. It was a highly sexist and very structured society, and colleges and universities reflected that environment.

College administrators were, by and large, white Christian males, generally Protestants, who had been effective academics and moved to the administrative ranks near the end of their professional careers. An individual's ethnic and religious backgrounds were important even into the 1950s. Colleges and universities with the exception of those in the Ivy League were sleepy backwaters with minimal effect on the rest of society.

Since much of higher education was not free, students who enrolled largely came from families with the financial means to pay for their education. A common adage for the time was, "College-bred was a four-year loaf made out of papa's dough." A college education was viewed as optional and largely for the benefit of the wealthy.

Students were influenced by where their parents or family members had gone to school or by their own church affiliation. Preference was given to children of alumni— legacy admissions as it is called today—and strict quotas were in place for various ethnic, religious, and racial minorities. Occasionally children of immigrants were admitted, but there were quotas placed on these groups to assure that they would not have significant influence on the academic environment. It was a time when prejudice, discrimination, and sexism were part of American society,

The Not-So-Recent Past

and universities, consciously or not, reflected those same views. During this era from the 1920s to the 1950s, student recruitment and retention were not pressing issues for academic institutions.

Administrators and faculty appeared unconcerned if students failed courses. In my first physics course, the professor said to the class, "Look to the right and look to the left. There will be only one of you three at the end of this course." There was little concern if courses or programs were demanding, or if students had difficulty adjusting to faculty expectations. Accountability for failure rested solely with the student. At the time, the university's attitude toward college students was as "children" not differing from that of society as a whole. Mostly, as the saying goes, children or students "were to be seen and not heard." As such, institutions acted in loco parentis, notifying parents if a student was failing or having other difficulties. The concept of student privacy was unimagined at that time. The faculty and administrators together ran a tight ship, commanding the utmost respect from students. Complaints by students, ombudsmen, and grievance procedures were a thing of the future, as was remedial education. And it was expected that most students would complete their college education over a four-year period— exceptions were few and far between.

Being an administrator in such an environment was not very demanding. Faculty and staff had low expectations in terms of salaries, research equipment, and supplies. Budgets, controlled solely by administrators, were modest due to the limited resources of most institutions. Personnel

Failed Grade

turnover was low, and, as with most individuals working in the private sector, faculty invariably stayed with the same institution until retirement. In effect, there was little mobility or interest in moving from one institution to another, not only because there was no clear advantage financially or professionally, but also because people felt more comfortable in an area where they were accepted and not viewed as outsiders. Geographic mobility occurred much later.

Faculty development was not usually a concern of academic administrators. Financial support for travel to professional meetings was the exception rather than the rule. If a faculty member wanted to go to a meeting, and it would not interfere with his teaching responsibilities, then it was possible. But the cost was always at the faculty member's expense. Research and other scholarly activities were neither encouraged nor discouraged at many institutions. It was left entirely to the interests of the faculty members themselves.

Attendance by faculty and administrators at graduation and other various institutional activities was mandatory. It was viewed as an academic responsibility since pomp and ceremony were part of the theater at every commencement. Replacement of faculty resided solely with the administrator. Committees for faculty recruitment were off in the future. In fact, it was common for institutions to tap former students for faculty positions. Typically, students who had performed well academically and lived in the area were the most likely candidates. In the event an institution needed to look beyond the pool of former students for a

The Not-So-Recent Past

faculty position, the administrator would simply contact former colleagues for recommendations. All that a potential junior faculty member needed was a recommendation from a former faculty member to secure a position. The administrator wanted to be certain new faculty members would "fit in" with the other faculty from the standpoint of religion and certainly race. This meant that there were few religious and ethnic minorities chosen.

Environment During and Following World War II

World War II brought many changes to society as a whole, but especially to higher education. During this period, three important events occurred that had a profound effect upon higher education. One of these took place during the war; the other two followed it.

1. Atomic Bomb Project

The first of these milestones was the so-called Manhattan Project[1,2]. It was a top-secret government project designed to create the first atomic bomb in order to win the war as rapidly as possible. Physicists, chemists, and engineers, as well as faculty from many colleges and universities with the requisite background and knowledge, were recruited for this project, centralized in Los Alamos, New Mexico. Its objective was to produce a sufficient amount of Uranium-235 and to determine whether a particular amount would generate a nuclear explosion.

Failed Grade

For the first time, higher education had great relevance to the community. Academia was perceived as a place where learning and educational background were not only important for secret government projects, but also for the education and training of students needed for the evolving military and industrial complex, in addition to the traditional liberal arts disciplines. Development of the atomic bomb was a crucial beginning of government support for research and scientific education in universities that has continued to the present.

This began the relationship between the federal government and universities, as well as the standards for academia and research. With the federal government interest in research, institutions began receiving financial support in the form of grants and contracts, as well as much-needed equipment and funds to help cover significant overhead costs. Faculty members began supplementing their teaching with academic pursuits of their own. This new direction complicated the academic environment from both a faculty and an administrative perspective. Administrators encouraged faculty to undertake government research since overhead support to the institution was provided with each grant. However, faculty engaged in such funded research had to balance their time between teaching and meeting their government commitments. Yet, this was a source of money to help educate students, especially those in graduate programs.

The Not-So-Recent Past

2. G.I. Bill

The second major impact upon academia and one that also provided resources to institutions was the G.I. Bill,[3] passed by Congress in June 1944 immediately before the war ended. This legislation gave veterans with limited financial resources, the opportunity to obtain a university education at the federal government's expense. Many men whose job opportunities were placed on hold during the war saw this period as a chance to obtain the knowledge and skills that would give them the background necessary to earn a decent living for themselves and their families.

Many of these men had lived through the Great Depression, making this goal even more imperative. They were now older and more mature than previous students. Many who were already married were anxious to make up for the time already lost by serving in the military. They viewed their college experience very seriously—with no time to engage in childish pranks and social activities.

When they arrived on college campuses, veterans were purposeful, with little tolerance for the pedantic and rigid environment permeating higher education. They raised questions regarding the curriculum and course sequence that had never before been posed by students. They did not view themselves as children, but rather as the adults they had become. These changes presented new challenges for both faculty and academic administrators alike. These veterans questioned why certain courses were required for their programs and others were not. They wanted greater involvement in determining what their education should be, not from the standpoint of making it easier but more

Failed Grade

substantive and relevant to what they wanted to do. They were no longer the passive students of the pre-war era; it was their education and they wanted a say in it.

3. Sputnik Era

During this time of turmoil, a third major influence on higher education in the United States occurred when the world became aware of Sputnik on October 4, 1957. Whereas the success of the Manhattan Project had promoted confidence and a feeling that American science and engineering were supreme and at the cutting edge of innovation, the early development of Sputnik and the space program by Russian scientists and engineers created great angst in the United States. Anxiety was exacerbated by the tension of the Cold War period, already well underway.

During this time, there was great introspection in the United States and skepticism about the country's ability to keep up with the technical advances being made around the world. One major focus was higher education and its importance in preparing a new generation for an evolving technological society. The result was a significant expansion of higher education, especially in science and engineering. The federal government supported this expansion when the National Defense Education Act[4] was passed by Congress and signed into law in 1958.

Higher education was viewed as important for national security reasons, and during this time, the great systems of state universities came into being. High school education was no longer considered an end in itself, but rather as a

8

The Not-So-Recent Past

preparation for the rigors of college education. The number of institutions increased exponentially, and there was a radical transformation as to how colleges and universities were being run. Many "normal" schools changed their charters, becoming state colleges. Their focus was no longer only preparing young women to teach in primary and secondary schools, but on preparing them for the many careers that beckoned. Women, who had worked in factories during the war, began to aspire for careers other than teaching or nursing. They no longer accepted career limitations based on their sex, marital status or whether they had children.

4. Higher Education's Role in America's Economy

Higher education had moved from being a sleepy backwater to a central component in preparing young people—both men and women—for many different roles in the workforce and the economy as a whole. And academic administrators had to find ways to cope with these major shifts in expectations and attitudes. As a result, colleges and universities became a focal point for changes in society.

Gaining a college degree was no longer viewed as a luxury, but as a necessity. Hence, the discrimination and bigotry of the past, where blacks were not accepted at many colleges, where there were enrollment quotas for Jews, and where Roman Catholics were discouraged from applying to some Ivy League schools, could no longer be condoned or tolerated. Academic administrators, who bore the responsibility for these enrollment barriers for minorities

Failed Grade

and women, were spurred by the government to remove them.

Through the passage of the Civil Rights Act (1964), the Equal Employment Opportunity Act (1972) and Americans with Disabilities Act (1990), institutions of higher education have evolved into a setting more tolerant of all differences. These changes have occurred not only in the undergraduate and graduate admissions processes, but also in recruiting for faculty and administrative positions. Though there remain inequities between various groups in terms of fair and adequate pay, the outcome and directions are clear: gender and ethnicity must not be factors in determining compensation.

5. Activism in Academia and the Vietnam War

In addition to access and equality of compensation, what was happening politically in society became important to colleges and universities and their constituencies. This was never more apparent than during the Vietnam War. The turbulence in society, generated by the Vietnam War, exploded onto college campuses. Students and faculty, as protesters, changed the environment on campuses for years to come. Much of this anti-war sentiment spilled into society, creating a new "zero tolerance" attitude toward government. With distrust in the air, the government was no longer free to engage in important political initiatives without popular support of the American people, many of whom were being educated in our colleges and universities.

Students and faculties in higher education had become an important constituency in American society. College

The Not-So-Recent Past

administrators, as well as state and federal governments, could no longer ignore the social concerns of students and faculties. Colleges and universities had become the intellectual centers of American society. The Vietnam War period ended the passivity of the past and ushered in a more socially-active era in which perceived injustices would be discussed and addressed on college campuses—with or without the consent of boards of trustees or university administrators. The environment had changed irrevocably.

The initial draft of this book was written prior to September 11, 2001. Though the full impact of this tragic event upon higher education remains unclear, it is already apparent that international students will be subject to greater scrutiny by government agencies than ever before. Consequently, fewer may be allowed on campuses, at least in the short run. Just how this event will impact enrollment and recruitment of students, faculty, and administrators and the academic environment remains to be seen.

Chapter Two
The New Financial Imperative

Growth of Higher Education

Over the intervening decades since the 1950s, a great deal has changed in higher education, but the most important change has been the growth in the number of institutions, the number of students attending programs in higher education, and the impact of colleges and universities on society and the economy. Higher education has undergone spectacular growth. Eric Gould, in his recent book, *The University in a Corporate Culture*, states,[1] "In 1950, there were some eighteen hundred American colleges and universities. In the next fifty years, that number doubled. Since 1980, the current-fund revenues of these institutions have increased three-fold, from over $65 billion to over $250 billion today. In 1900, twenty-nine thousand degrees were awarded; fifty years later the number had reached nearly half a million. In 1995, more than 2 million

Failed Grade

people received some kind of college or university degree, and in 2000 the number reached 2,265,600."

In response to these developments and changing societal expectations, Ronald Corwin, a former sociology professor at Ohio State University writing thirty years ago, said that colleges and universities have become,[2] "complex, bureaucratic organizations, and they have been saddled with a wide range of goals that cannot possibly be effectively accommodated within the existing structures. Universities have been pressured by their local constituents and, more recently, by the federal government to provide technical services to government and industry, to train workers for technical jobs, and to undertake basic and applied scientific research. Research foundations and government agencies have penetrated deep into the universities, impelling major administrative changes. Universities increasingly have come under scrutiny of state legislatures and government agencies; these are anxious that monies being spent on higher education are adequately accounted for and that colleges and universities are being administrated in an efficient manner. Their response to these pressures has been to develop bureaucratic procedures that have aggravated other problems."

Transformation from Collegial to Corporate Structure

In addition to the bureaucratic problems, colleges and universities have been transformed from a collegial to a corporate structure. Corporate or business models don't just apply anymore to companies in the private sector but have

The New Financial Imperative

influenced how nonprofit and educational institutions function today. Recently, a number of other books and articles have been written about the corporate developments in higher education.[3-7]

Business speak is the lingua franca of the day and affects every organization. Terms such as "CEO/COO," "brand name," "bottom line," "profit center," "value added," and "top down" are commonly used in all segments of society including higher education, effectively transforming colleges and universities into businesses. The major difference between a corporate and a collegial structure is that the latter involves shared governance between faculty and administration, requiring concurrence of both in major decisions. In a corporate structure, all decisions are initiated and made by administrators without requiring consensual faculty approval.

Why is that a bad environment for academia, one might ask? The objective of any corporation is to make money and to be profitable. An e-mail I received from Trinity College, will illustrate the point and show how the drive to profitability is influencing higher education. It was entitled, "Obtain the degree you may have already earned!"

"Privately accredited online college issues degrees based upon review of your employment and academic record, no classes or tests to take. Improve your career earning power by over 100-200% with a Bachelor, Master or Ph.D. obtained in as little as 30 days and for as little as a dinner out a few times for a month. Degree is accepted by 96% of companies today and we offer free lifetime

Failed Grade

verification services and optional transcripts for those students who require an official record."

Trinity is not alone in this activity. Corporate structure, financial imperatives, and rewards for entrepreneurial activities are not confined to online universities but have become pronounced at many eminent institutions without any widespread discussion regarding its merit. The growing emphasis on materialism in society is permeating even the so-called "ivory towers" where students formerly focused on learning for learning's sake; where the priority of the faculty was educating the next generation and preparing it to function in a changing world. Unfortunately, materialism is driving many institutions and their faculties where entrepreneurship is valued at the expense of educating students.

Faculty and Administrators in New Paradigm

With the boundaries between colleges and the outside material world becoming blurred, faculty are no longer judged by the standards set and performances achieved by their students nor even the quality of their own scholarship but by how successful they are in generating external support for their research. Money and entrepreneurship are the important benchmarks. Similarly, success in generating money, equivalent to a corporation's yearly increase in earnings, is also the key measure of the effectiveness of academic administrators. Money now reigns supreme, and the amount is readily quantifiable.

Some university presidents have stated publicly that academic institutions should model themselves after

The New Financial Imperative

Fortune 500 companies, adopting industry buzzwords and slogans such as "Quality is Job One," even though schools are educating people, not producing things. A corporation has far different objectives and constraints from those in higher education. For one, the personnel budget in colleges and universities can be 90 percent or greater, and of this, the bulk of the expenditure involves faculty, many of whom are tenured. Therefore, education is very labor intensive, not readily amenable to cost containment and "downsizing" achievable in industry since tenured faculty cannot be fired unless the institution is experiencing financial exigency. People, the environment they create, and the knowledge they impart and scholarship they perform, are academia's greatest assets. If you downsize people, then clearly you're cutting into the unique thing that academia has to offer.

Even given the differences between the corporate world and academic settings, some academic leaders argue that using industrial models may be highly beneficial. At the heart of this argument is the narrow focus on each program's ability to function as a profit center much like a business. This shift in thinking has led to a short-term focus on results, with little thought for the long-term success of the institution as a whole or even on the ultimate success rates of its students. And much like the corporate world, the faculty and administrators, who make large contributions to an institution's "bottom line," reap the biggest rewards in terms of salaries and recognition. Effective teaching, never easy to measure for the present much less the future, becomes low on the totem pole in such an environment.

Failed Grade

Collegiate Athletics

The first sign of corporate policy creeping into academics began with its application to collegiate athletic programs. At one time, athletic programs were simply viewed as important, but extracurricular—peripheral to the main mission of institutions. Over time, however, football and basketball programs, in particular, have become big business at many schools. This transformation has been fueled not just by the interest of students, but mainly by the pocketbooks of wealthy alumni, local and national media, and corporate advertisers. Even the entertainment industry is getting in on the act now[8-11] by providing significant revenue for the privilege of televising games.

As James Duderstadt says,[8] "In the 1960s and 1970s, these spectator events turned into public entertainment on a national scale, with television as the driving force." Coaches and athletic directors who shepherd winning teams are rewarded at financial levels that cannot be compared with others who teach at the same institution. Significant support is derived not only from radio and television stations but also by advertising contracts and of course, the alumni. College stadiums and arenas now resemble those in professional sports, with their corporate boxes and the special treatment afforded only to those able to pay for such amenities. College sports programs are now in the entertainment business, overshadowing the importance of academics.

College sports are being challenged by corruptive influences. As James Duderstadt states,[9] "Particularly serious is the impact of gambling on the integrity of

The New Financial Imperative

intercollegiate athletics. ... not only does gambling undermine the values of higher education, but it brings with it elements of our society, including organized crime, that can pose great danger to our students and our institutions." Institutions, once tarnished, have great difficulty regaining their former pristine character.

Until the past twenty-five years or so, faculty members were responsible for ensuring the integrity of college athletic programs, which were viewed as an integral part of the entire academic program. On one occasion in 1962, the faculty at Ohio State University voted against its football team participating in the Rose Bowl, viewing it as inimical to the academic interests of the institution and its students. As a result of the vote, the team didn't go that year—a phenomenon that would be unheard of today.

Today, faculty members are largely uninvolved in athletic programs. These programs are separate and overseen by the president, the athletic director, and individuals directly responsible to them. To demonstrate how disconnected athletic programs are from the rest of the institution, coaches and directors move fluidly from college to professional programs, and vice versa, at salary levels that exceed most prized faculty members or, in many cases, even those of university presidents. Regardless of what administrators say, the sole goal of college athletics is to win. The objective of educating students has taken a back seat to increasing ad revenues, TV contracts, and filling stadiums and arenas each season. Derek Bok, in his recent book, *Universities In The Marketplace — The Commercialization of Higher Education*, spends a great

Failed Grade

deal of time on this subject, and university presidents have become enmeshed with sports recruiting problems on campus, as at the University of Colorado recently.

Coaches not producing winning teams are summarily replaced, even if they must be paid the remainder of a multi-year salary contract. An administration may pay lip service to the low graduation rates of a team's student athletes, but often a coach's termination has more to do with his or her failure to put more games in the "win" column. Winning has become as important in academic settings as it is in the corporate world, making education far less important than the entertainment value "student" athletes provide for other students, alumni, politicians, corporate sponsors, and the general public.

Entrepreneurship and Conflicts in Academic Programs

The preoccupation with generating money is no longer confined to athletic programs, but is also affecting administrators and faculty in academic programs. One of the main roles of the college administrator is to create and increase an institution's endowment. Obviously, obtaining such external resources can be beneficial in providing scholarship support for students, capital to construct new buildings and to renovate existing facilities, professorships for faculty, and computers and other equipment for the institution.

However, raising money should not be the primary role of the president and other senior academic administrators. But as academic institutions have attempted to implement

The New Financial Imperative

more business concepts into the environment, fundraising has overshadowed administrators' commitments to students, faculty and program development. Success in fundraising is how senior administrators are now evaluated.

In my own experience as a dean at Ohio State University from 1977-88, I was successful in generating financial support for the college from alumni and industry. However, I have known excellent administrators who were highly effective in program development and staff recruiting, but were not superb fundraisers. These individuals, once highly valued in academia, are no longer being recognized in the current climate. One merely needs to examine the credentials of current candidates for president to realize that business and political connections are much more important than academic accomplishments.

The fact that many senior administrators spend as much as 50 percent of their time fundraising sends a clear message to faculty in their institution that this activity is very important. A faculty member's job description varies widely and depends not only on a specific college or university, but also on a professor's specific discipline. For instance, a small liberal arts college, with its primary focus on undergraduate education, has clearly different expectations of its faculty than a large, multi-faceted university, where educating graduate students and post-doctoral fellows is part of a faculty member's responsibilities.

Faculty who teach in certain disciplines are expected to spend a greater portion of their time seeking outside grants for their own salaries as well as assistance for students. For

Failed Grade

instance, those who teach in the physical, chemical, and biomedical sciences—where external support for research is available from government and private agencies—are expected to prepare and submit grant proposals so that their programs can provide stipends to graduate students, post-doctoral fellows, and research assistants. By comparison, outside support for social science programs (i.e., arts and languages) is generally scarce, thereby allowing faculty who teach in these disciplines to focus more on their students as well as their own scholarship and research.

In my experience teaching in the biomedical science area, faculty members who generate large amounts of grant and contract monies for their institution are considered the most valuable and are rewarded with higher salary increases. There are clear salary differentials between faculty with outside funding potential and those who may not have such opportunities. To attract and retain faculty with the highest potential for generating grant funds, institutions lure new faculty members with support packages for research, often valued in the hundreds of thousands of dollars.

Such faculty incentives, called "start-up costs," are becoming increasingly more widespread as a recruiting tool. Even faculty members just beginning their academic careers expect to receive such packages for research when they arrive on campus. And it is expected that they will be successful in getting external support for their research.

The New Financial Imperative

Show Me the Money

The rules for academic survival and advancement have changed dramatically. The "publish or perish" motto of a previous generation has been replaced with "show me the money." While publishing still remains an important factor in academia because it provides justification to obtain further support for new grants and contracts, an academician's ability to generate money is his or her ticket to job security, promotion, and high salaries.

When a faculty member receives a grant, especially from a government agency, a percentage of this grant goes to the institution for "overhead expenses." These funds, amounting to as much as 50 percent of the total grant, are not necessarily available to the faculty member unless authorized by senior administrators. Some may go back to the individual, the department, and the college. However, it is not uncommon for an administrator to allocate a portion of these funds for activities such as graduate student programs, secretarial and administrative positions, travel, facilities maintenance, or pet initiatives. Given the amounts of overhead money acquired by some institutions, it is not surprising that a few administrators are tempted to misuse funds for their own purposes. An outrageous use of government monies that was targeted to support research led to the resignation of a president at a prestigious university in California. Accountability as to how overhead monies are spent is a current problem affecting many universities.

Although it may be a necessary activity, the continual drive for obtaining overhead monies is corrupting

Failed Grade

institutions and diverting educators from their primary mission: to educate students. And when an institution seeks money for anything other than benefiting students, faculty and the rest of the academic enterprise, it is apparent the institution has lost its way. Some professors, who might be top-rate teachers and devoted to educating students, may be considered second-rate only because they are not bringing money into their departments. Naturally, with the distraction of fundraising, educating students becomes less important, regardless of what the institutions say.

I have known very talented faculty members who have had difficulty in generating funds simply because their area of research was not in vogue at the time they were seeking federal funding. Dr. Judah Folkman, Andrus Professor of Pediatric Surgery and Professor of Cell Biology at Harvard University, found in the early stages of his research on the importance of angiogenesis in tumor growth that he couldn't get government funding for his research. He said, "I have a closet full of rejected proposals." After his ideas were validated and their importance in controlling tumor growth was appreciated, he observed "my critics became my competitors."

Some faculty members are not well-funded researchers but are sensitive individuals, caring deeply for students, and are very effective in placing them in exciting careers. Many are wonderful colleagues with high academic standards and should be greatly valued for their contribution to higher education. Conversely, I have seen faculty who were poor colleagues and treated students as mere vassals, but were effective in generating external financial support. Teaching

The New Financial Imperative

was a low priority for some, but because they possessed entrepreneurial skills, they received the highest recognition from administrators. I knew one dean who was fired from his administrative position because he didn't recommend a faculty member for promotion. The faculty member was effective in generating research dollars but was a poor teacher. The dean felt both were important; the provost did not.

In addition, tenured faculty in some disciplines, whose full salary is committed by the institution, are expected by administrators to place increasing percentages of their salaries on grants and contracts. The plan is euphemistically called "salary recovery." Those who can generate enough money to cover their entire salary either directly or by overhead monies are prized. In effect, such faculty members are considered to be working for "free" since the institution has no financial commitment to them for that year.

With policies like "salary recovery" in place, an institution's funds, once earmarked for salaries, are freed for other uses, determined by the senior administrator. Though at first blush this would appear to be desirable, such faculty members are in effect working for the granting agency, "buying" themselves out of teaching and their need to deal with students. Institutions may pride themselves on being capable of evaluating student performance, but leave to external agencies with resources the evaluation and importance of faculty scholarship.

Failed Grade

Faculty as Business Consultants and Executives

A second area of concern related to the financial imperative is the trend toward faculty becoming involved in private-sector businesses such as consulting and commercial enterprises. Many institutions allow faculty members to consult as much as one day out of the five-day academic week. The rationale for allowing faculty to participate in private-sector enterprises is that they can acquire valuable information and "real-world" experience that can be brought back into the classroom or the laboratory and shared with students. Arguably, such knowledge can and does benefit students since exposure to practical applications might enhance their placement in positions after graduation.

However, since faculty consulting is lucrative, it can lead to abuse raising ethical issues. I knew a full professor at M.I.T. who was instrumental, along with several colleagues, in forming a technical company. As the company developed, he realized more of his time would be required than one day per week. So he left his tenured position to devote his full energies to the fledgling company. Knowing his commitment to his business venture would require more time than allowed, my colleague acted responsibly by not abusing the great freedom an academic position provides. He also acted out of respect for his students, who would have suffered had he tried to juggle his business venture with his academic duties. When his commitment to the company ended and he wanted to return to academia, he did so at another university.

The New Financial Imperative

Regrettably, some faculty members are not as ethical as this former colleague. Another individual, who was being recruited for the chair of a bioengineering department, made as a condition for accepting the appointment his continued operation of a startup company he had launched. This stipulation raises a host of dilemmas. For instance, what would be his priority should he decide to recruit students to work for him—the students' education or the company's bottom line? Where would the line between the institution end and the company begin? Would the institution have a vested interest in the company, and how would the priority of educating students fit into the overall equation? Would he be receptive to other faculty in his department doing the same thing?

While these were issues related to one specific situation, it seems more and more that these are some of the thorny issues that must be sorted out as the new academic/industrial complexes are being created in universities.[12] Bok, in his book *Universities In The Marketplace—The Commercialization of Higher Education*, states,[13] "Corporate research support will also require the university to accept a certain amount of secrecy since companies will naturally wish to avoid having valuable findings from the work they fund fall into the hands of competitors. From the standpoint of the university and of science itself; however, secrecy has several unfortunate results. It disrupts collegial relationships when professors cannot talk freely to other members of their department. It erodes trust, as members of scientific conferences wonder whether other participants are

Failed Grade

withholding information for commercial reasons. It promotes waste as scientists needlessly duplicate work that other investigators have already performed in secret for business reasons. Worst of all, secrecy may retard the course of science itself, since progress depends upon every researcher being able to build upon the findings of other investigators." In higher education today, the obsession with money ripples through campus operations and policies.

Tuition and Academic Standards

Another area, which is not so readily apparent, is student retention. The importance of tuition dollars—generated from students, the state, or both—has created a climate at some state institutions where fewer students are failed, regardless of academic performance. At the same time, qualified out-of-state and foreign students are more heavily recruited since their tuition is higher.

Increasingly, students have become equated with income. The thinking is: the more students passed and retained, the more money generated by the institution. Such views put faculty members under increasing pressure to pass a higher percentage of students. As a consequence, there has been significant grade inflation over the past fifteen years. Fewer students are being awarded a grade of "D" or being failed. The lowest grade at some places is a "C"—even for those who are marginal at best.

Even some prestigious institutions have succumbed to this pressure, as noted by the president of Harvard, Lawrence H. Summers, when asked, "Grade inflation is

The New Financial Imperative

rampant at Harvard. Some 90% of all students now graduate with honors. Should they?" He replied, "Standard-setting is integral to education, and grading is integral to standard-setting. What grades and honors represent (that an honors student) is the best relative to a peer group at a point in time. People run much faster than they used to, but we still give only one gold medal."[14]

Perhaps more disturbing than grade inflation itself is that faculty, attempting to take a stand against it, may find their courses assigned to those more amenable to the changing environment. Grade inflation is not generally discussed on college campuses, but administrative expectations are readily apparent. The corporate environment has only exacerbated this trend.

Political Concerns with Graduation Rates

Concern with graduation rates is provided not only by students, their parents, and administrators, but also by politicians who have begun to question the dropout and low four-year graduation rates at state supported institutions. Of special concern are student athletes. Since the political establishment has an important say in funding state institutions, its views are given serious administrative consideration.

Many politicians assume that if graduation rates are low, an institution's academic expectations may be un-reasonable, accounting for the noticeable attrition rates, especially among student athletes. The latter have a greater interest in entering the professional sports world rather than completing their college educations. And those realizing

29

Failed Grade

they will not have a professional sports career may have little incentive to remain in college.

Encouraging the lowering of academic expectations translates into everyone being entitled to a degree or license, regardless of performance. That policy would ultimately have a disastrous effect not only upon the quality of those graduating from colleges and universities but also on the entire society. This is a marked change from how colleges functioned historically when no one was ever guaranteed a degree; it had to be earned. The concern for low graduation rates applies not only to student athletes, but also to those in some demanding science and engineering programs. Many in these programs take longer than four years to complete. Administrators and state agencies are questioning the reasons for such statistics.

One assumption is the lack of a student-friendly environment. Perhaps the number of credit hours and courses required for graduation should be reduced, even though these programs have been in operation for decades. Such a trend is occurring but the reasons may be more financial than anything else. Science and engineering programs that are shorter will probably attract more students and gain greater market share, but this will not be the best thing for science and engineering as a whole or for society because scrimping on education is no answer.

One final example illustrates the importance of the financial imperative. A former colleague of mine had been a dean at a university and decided to return to the faculty at the same institution. Several years later, he decided to

The New Financial Imperative

apply for the deanship at another institution. As part of the recruiting process, the college's president interviewed him.

The president told him that the length of the program in that college was being increased to provide for experiential education at various hospitals. Obviously, this is labor intensive and requires adequate sites and faculty for educating students. When my former colleague indicated to the president that the number of students admitted to the program would depend on the number of faculty and experiential sites available (certainly an understandable requirement), the president became incensed. It seems he viewed this program as a "cash cow" and for enrollment to be tied to academic "needs" was deemed unacceptable.

Students were equated with income and enrollment had to be maximized at whatever cost. If the experiential program became substandard, then so be it. Needless to say, my former colleague lost interest in the position and withdrew his application.

Of course, no one wants a marginal physician or other health care provider attending to critical needs. Society assumes that a degree attests to an individual's competence—anything less places the public at risk. Thus, we are dependent upon the integrity of faculty and administrators to ensure that grades have a meaningful relationship to a student's future performance. Anything less is unethical.

Where the corporate structure and its financial imperative have primacy over academic standards, there are serious implications. If everything is geared to generating money, whether it be administrators focusing on

31

Failed Grade

endowment and fundraising, or faculty whose entrepreneurial skills are valued over their teaching and involvement with students, or the retention of marginal students, regardless of academic performance, we have a situation with long-term consequences. All have one thread in common: the financial imperative. One hopes such a result where established in colleges and universities will be reversed. Higher education's value to society and to future generations of students, faculty, and administrators is just too important to be jeopardized by such a trend.

Chapter Three
The Organization

Organizational Structure

As Ronald Corwin stated,[1] "American institutions of higher learning have involved an incredibly complex governance structure over the past century. Many of their problems today stem from the way they are organized and internally controlled. No aspect of the modern university is more complex than the way it is controlled." Though this statement was made thirty years ago, it is relevant today. Universities have always been bureaucratic, but with the increase of federal and state mandates, the ease of litigation, the proliferation of relationships with industry, and the creation of a corporate structure, administrative activities have undergone a remarkable change. The most visible signs of higher education's corporate culture are the types of individuals selected for senior administrative positions and their roles in the organization. Such changes may not have occurred as dramatically in smaller colleges

Failed Grade

and universities, but in larger or mega-universities focused on research and securing of external support for a variety of activities, the corporate structure is readily apparent. At smaller colleges, the major focus appears to remain on educating the next generation. In mega-universities, presidents now view themselves as CEOs with full responsibility for all decision making and activities and perquisites that go with the title. Presidents in a previous era were considered the senior academic officers and peers of the faculty. They spent most of their time on campus, relating to faculty, staff, and students, in contrast with how presidents now spend their time off campus in fundraising and political roles. In fact, the president's home was generally on campus to facilitate interacting with campus constituents.

At the same time, a university provost or vice president for academic affairs has become the COO, responsible for the day-to-day operations of the institution while the president is away from campus raising money and making political connections to achieve that objective. In an article entitled, "Academics on Board—University Presidents as Corporate Directors," Nancy P. Goldschmidt and James H. Finkelstein in *Academe* said,[2] "Today, a university president's activities are more closely linked to the outside world than in the past." Now presidents' major focus is activities designed to generate financial resources.

In these powerful roles, Robert C. and Jon Solomon state[3] in their book, *Up the University—Recreating Higher Education in America*, "administrators come to think of themselves as the university, just as corporate management

The Organization

has come to think of itself as the corporation." And, as in most corporations, senior-level university administrators have clearly defined job descriptions, with salaries tied to the size of the budget and responsibilities for the specific areas they oversee. So the model of administrators with responsibilities, overseeing numerous departments, has given way to an increasing bureaucracy with a trend toward creating single-function officers. The end result: administrative costs, as a percentage of an institution's total costs, have risen more sharply at the expense of academic programs.

When administrative costs increase under this model, institutions either have to generate more funds to continue existing programs, reduce program support, or explore the simpler solution, namely raising tuition. That is one of the reasons tuitions have increased faster than the average inflation rate. Given that senior administrators are now focused so narrowly on protecting an institution's "bottom line" and prestige at any costs, many institutions have hired staff in Washington, D.C., to monitor legislation that could have ramifications for higher education. These individuals lobby on behalf of the university, based on its own financial agenda, while also keeping top administrators abreast of issues that could impact higher education and add to institutional costs. Like any of the nation's powerful lobbies, collectively they can help defeat legislation that could have financial consequences for their institutions.

At the same time, university personnel at state capitals monitor state and local government activity for potential legislation and political concerns that might affect tuition

Failed Grade

policies, new capital projects, and a focus on graduation rates. Also important are intellectual property issues that could hinder research efforts on campuses and impact the developing "academic-industrial" complex.

The laissez-faire philosophy of administrators in the past has been replaced by direct involvement in the legislative process. To influence legislation effectively, university presidents join corporate boards. In their article,[2] Goldschmidt and Finkelstein found, "About one-third of the presidents (from "top universities") served on one to five corporate boards: more than half were presidents of public universities.... In 2000, 60 percent of the presidents served on only one board, 24 percent on two boards, and 15 percent on from three to five boards." Important business people have easier access to governors and members of the state legislature. At the same time, such corporate board positions are highly lucrative. And thus salaries of university presidents are considerably greater than the amount actually provided by the institution itself.

The Academic-Industrial-Political Complex

Such activities contribute to creating the so-called "academic-industrial complex." As Eyal Press and Jennifer Washburn in their article entitled "The Kept University," (published March 2000 in *The Atlantic Monthly*) state,[4] "In higher education today corporations not only sponsor a growing amount of research—they frequently dictate the terms under which it is conducted. Professors, their image as unbiased truth-seekers notwithstanding, often own stock of the companies that fund their work. And universities

The Organization

themselves are exhibiting a markedly more commercial bent. Most now operate technology-licensing offices to manage their patent portfolios, often guarding their intellectual property as aggressively as any business would. Schools with limited budgets are pouring money into commercially-oriented fields of research, while downsizing humanities departments and curbing expenditures on teaching."

The cozy relationships between university presidents, politicians, and corporate officers in the business community have benefits for these powerful people. University presidents get appointed to corporate boards, transportation on company jets, and stay at plush hotels. Politicians and corporate officers become adjunct faculty after retirement. Some, with no academic experience, are selected as university presidents—especially politicians. They obtain special health care at university medical centers, choice seats for athletic events at the university and especially for bowl games, an important "say" in who is appointed to university boards of trustees, what names are used on new campus buildings, and who receives honorary degrees and other awards from the institution. It is an incestuous relationship benefiting the participants. Of course, all of this requires presidents to be away from campuses for long stretches of time, making them unavailable to deal with faculty, students, academic and infrastructure issues, as well as strategic planning for the institution.

As in any business, the successful institution must focus on potential sources of income and how these can be

Failed Grade

tapped. Since universities are nonprofit entities whose graduates do not directly contribute to the "bottom line," fundraising has become a significant and continuing endeavor for every nonprofit entity, including those in higher education. This is the case now even with those institutions that are state supported, as state legislatures increasingly reduce educational support as part of budgetary cutbacks.

Fundraising and Public Relations by Universities

Raising money has become a major role for university presidents, even at institutions with huge endowments,[5] such as Harvard and Yale, where the continuing financial need has not been clearly articulated. Acquisition of money has become an end in itself. And the most successful university presidents are those who are the most aggressive in this regard. This is indicative of how the organization has changed.

While the roles of senior administrators have changed dramatically over the years, so has the role of alumni organizations in a university setting. The president's role in the organization is to establish useful relationships with alumni, especially those of means, who can make important financial contributions to the institution. In this regard, alumni organizations provide an essential bridge between alumni and the institution. Alumni travel programs are designed, certainly in part, to determine alumni with the financial wherewithal to contribute to the university endowment and new building campaigns. Graduation anniversaries are celebrated faithfully, since that is a time

The Organization

for encouraging graduates to make financial pledges. Endowments provide the institution with a flow of funds during the donor's lifetime and even after the individual's death.

The president's role and effectiveness as fundraising manager now means more than academic credentials or concern for the institution's future direction. As a result, many universities have individuals with mediocre or nonexistent academic credentials occupying prestigious positions as heads of colleges and universities. Presidents with a vision of where higher education should be tomorrow are seldom to be found because the selection process[6] works against them. Short-term interests now drive the organization's focus, just as they do many for-profit corporations.

Modern-day presidents are highly skilled in public relations matters and attempt to stay "ahead of the curve" in predicting issues that the political establishment will focus on in the future.[7] It matters little how such issues can be translated to education—or even whether they should be. It is crucial that the institution's public image be viewed as "progressive," always on the "correct" side of important social issues. If the president is mainly a public relations fundraiser, addressing matters external to the institution, then, it's fair to ask, who is minding the day-to-day matters?

Provost as Chief Operating Officer

More and more, the role of operating the institution is falling to the provost or vice president for academic

Failed Grade

affairs—in effect, the chief operating officer (COO) as well as the fiscal officer in the organization. As the COO of any company, a provost is concerned with managing the organization and ensuring it runs smoothly when the president is away from campus on frequent trips. Though faculty search committees are responsible for recommending appropriate candidates to the president for the position of provost, the president, when the person is an internal candidate, decides who should apply and who will be appointed.

The provost is responsible for the academic programs and selection of college and university deans, department chairs, and program directors. And, along with the president, a provost decides which new programs can be added and those that should be downsized or terminated. In partnership with the fiscal officer, a provost is also instrumental in allocating resources and in determining the budget for various academic colleges and departments. In the past, the budgets allocated for these units were based on their academic quality, their ability to attract and retain the best students and faculty, and their academic contributions to the institution and its national recognition. The department's accomplishments, as well as the unique needs of individual programs, were important factors in determining resource allocation—an approach to budgets that is much less important now.

In today's approach, modeled more after the corporate world, a department's annual budget is based on revenue generation from student tuition, research grants, etc., minus any amounts to be used to cover general and administrative

The Organization

(G&A) expenses of the institution. The justification of the budget is determined on purely objective and measurable factors, making it a "fair" process for everyone involved. Of course, there are always exceptions. But in essence, each department is expected to manage its own financial "bottom line," regardless of cost differentials among programs.

In large part, this business model has taken hold at many universities, with income and financial accountability residing at the department level. The roles of the president, the provost, and the chief fiscal officer are to make everyone toe the corporate line of the organization. To ensure loyalty to upper administration, administrators below the provost, such as deans and department chairs, are generally rewarded with significant pay differentials, compared with faculty members in their units. This was not the case in previous times. As with any corporate structure, decisions are made at the top and do not necessarily require the consensus of subordinates, of faculty and staff. People still mention the philosophy of shared decision making. But in reality, those administrators with budgeting responsibilities are making decisions. It is a "top-down" structure. Budgetary control and decision making go hand in hand, since there must be administrative accountability and control.

Academic Governance

A relevant example showing how far along in the corporate culture universities have come is reported[8] by Derek Bok in his book *Universities in the Marketplace—*

41

Failed Grade

The Commercialization of Higher Education. He reports a decision made unilaterally by a dean of one of the prestigious business schools in the country. "At Columbia University, Dean Feldberg's decision to have his Business School collaborate with the Internet education company (U.Next) was taken without any discussion with the faculty. 'I made the decision,' Feldberg said. 'I didn't take it to the faculty.' 'I saw the opportunity to participate in the market value of this company and to increase the endowment of the school.'" So much for shared governance.

Faculty meetings used to be for decisions to be made jointly by faculty and administrators. They have become perfunctory and for informational purposes only. Consequently, department and all-college meetings are becoming less relevant and not as widely attended as they once were since major decisions are not generally made there. Still, faculty members retain a measure of responsibility for faculty recruitment, promotion, and tenure, and generally for program development and approval. While faculty influence has not been totally eroded, there are new college initiatives proposed by administrators on a regular basis that exclude faculty input as cited above.

Tenure and Managing Institutional Costs

Increasingly in the corporate university, attempts are made to eliminate tenure positions and replace them with term appointments. This issue will be discussed in greater depth in Chapter 6, "Faculty and Tenure Matters." The advantage from an institutional perspective is to provide

The Organization

administrators with increased control over future costs and their ability to eliminate programs together with the requisite faculty or staff without legal complications. Tenure is viewed as an impediment in a corporate organization. Arguments presented by administrators dwell upon faculty members who have become "dead wood" and are no longer educationally relevant. Another argument states there is a need for "clinical" faculty even in departments and units that are not health related. But the real issue is limiting future costs by reducing or eliminating permanent positions.

A related development is increasing the time needed to achieve tenure. The reason given is to permit faculty longer time to demonstrate value to the tenure-granting unit. But when the increase is from five to seven years to eleven, the objective is to keep faculty members in a probationary period for a longer time. Probationary faculty can be terminated readily with less cause than those who have achieved tenure. And that may be the real objective.

With replacement of tenured and senior faculty members by junior, clinical, and preferably part-time faculty members at a lower salary and without benefits, the institution has limited its long-term financial responsibility. The focus is controlling expenditures, and since faculty and staff account frequently for more than 90 percent of a unit's budget, this item would be subject to greater administrative control. The corporate structure does not want to be saddled with future expenditures over which it has little control, tenure being a major limitation in this regard.

Failed Grade

While the corporate structure has not fully spread to areas beyond central administration, the trend is apparent, as shown by the Columbia Business School. The structure and organization of departments are beginning to emulate the levels above them. Once an easy "open door" policy, faculty and staff accessibility to department chairs and college deans—extending even to presidents and provosts—now requires scheduling appointments in advance as well as providing a precise reason for needing to see an individual.

An example comes to mind. A faculty member had known her department chair for numbers of years since she had been one of his major professors. That is not an unusual situation in colleges. For personal reasons and because of their long association, she was able to see him quickly when she wanted to share a particular personal issue. As she was leaving the appointment, the departmental secretary told her that, in future meetings with the chair, she would need to be accompanied by the unit director who was responsible for the budget in her particular area of study/research.

The chair wanted to avoid situations where he might be asked to respond to requests in the absence of the administrator to whom this person was reporting. The once-collegial environment on campuses now reeks of bureaucratic "red tape." People have become "cogs" in the corporate structure, making their way through the required chain of command.

The Organization

Bureaucratic Overgrowth

Increased number of staff and administrators relative to faculty supports the contention that the university bureaucracy has gotten worse. And while at one time the goal may have been to increase organizational efficiency, certainly no one is arguing that it's been successful. On the contrary, the university has become patently less efficient and more administrators carry out duties peripheral to the educational mission of a particular institution.

Some of these individuals include personnel hired to assist in fundraising and alumni activities, provide support for the maintenance of computers and other technical equipment, assist in student recruitment and retention, deal with purchasing and various budgetary matters, assist and monitor diversity initiatives, and check compliance with federal and state mandates. Increased institutional costs result from such mandates but are not funded by federal and state government. While the roles of such people may seem important, many times they add to administrative bureaucracy and hinder efficiency (especially given that newly recruited, nonacademic personnel are so narrowly focused on single issues, with less on their job plates than ever). In a corporate climate, it is easier to justify hiring new administrative assistants, especially when budgetary responsibility has become totally an administrative prerogative.

This contrasts with corporations where both management and stockholders have a vested interest in seeing that administrative expenses are kept low. Profitable companies monitor their overhead expenses carefully since these

Failed Grade

directly impact a company's profitability and "bottom line." In academic institutions there is no such discipline. No countervailing efforts or groups are responsible for reining in unbridled administrative growth since the administrator, controlling the budget, determines how the resources are to be spent. Administrative travel and hiring of additional personnel are determined solely by the administrator in charge. I knew one dean who used the college budget for his travel to professional meetings, while there were no funds to send faculty to important scientific meetings. Resources can be spent unwisely and replenished by yet another tuition hike. This is the legacy of the corporate structure.

It has produced a chimera, an organization without the controls existing in profit-making companies and yet with some of the undesired features of a corporation. Boards of trustees, the ultimate governing authorities in academic institutions, frequently lack the knowledge or expertise to question how budgets and administrative priorities are determined by the president and provost. As faculty governance has decreased, the board's role has become of more critical importance within colleges and universities.

Chapter Four
Boards of Trustees

Function of the Board
Boards of trustees are traditionally the governing bodies whose responsibilities are to set policy and direction for colleges and universities. They are the ultimate authority for appointing administrators and faculty; the decision makers in awarding tenure and granting promotions; and the approvers of the institution's budget, tuition, and salary increases and oversight of the institution's endowment funds. The board decides which academic programs will be instituted and which are to be terminated and approves the purchase and sale of property and the modification of existing facilities as well as the construction of new facilities. The board is the academic counterpart to the board of directors in the commercial sector and, as such, has considerable responsibility in the governance and functioning of the institution.

Failed Grade

Credentials of Board Members

With such authority, what should the credentials be for individuals serving in this important role, and how are their actions monitored? Members of boards of trustees at colleges and universities have been invariably selected for past contributions to the institution, not their knowledge of higher education. At state institutions, in particular, politicians tend to appoint individuals who have supported them in political campaigns, with prestigious appointments serving as "paybacks." At private colleges, individuals selected to serve on boards of trustees frequently have made significant financial contributions to the institution and are beholden to the president for their appointment. The president's expectation is they will continue to contribute to the institution's financial needs.

These positions are largely honorary from a standpoint of knowledge, with no real requirement that board members possess the background or skills to engage in serious policy-making decisions. Instead, these are left to the president, provost, and senior faculty. Under the old collegial structure, there was effective interplay among academicians so that the board's ceremonial and financial roles were tolerable. In today's more corporate structure, however, where faculty members are being marginalized in policy-making decisions, the board's understanding of the academic enterprise and the inner workings of the institution have become more important.

The current selection process for appointing board members is outmoded and arcane. When higher education was of marginal importance to the general society, it didn't

Boards of Trustees

matter who occupied these positions because the president, usually an established scholar, had grown up in the institution and knew how it functioned. However, as higher education has become more important to society and presidents are selected from a national pool with little direct knowledge of their institutions, the board's role in monitoring the effectiveness of the president and staff, as well as setting future directions, has become crucial. Yet, these boards continue to be populated with individuals with little knowledge or understanding of problems in higher education.[1]

In most instances, newly appointed members' understanding of higher education is limited to their experiences as undergraduates, dating back forty years, when college campuses were dramatically different and they were students. Few have any experience in higher education as either faculty or administrators. As a society, we wouldn't tolerate a medical board without physicians, a legal board without lawyers, a pharmacy board without pharmacists, or a plumbing board without plumbers. Yet, we readily accept boards of higher education without any academicians!

Students are even permitted on boards, but faculty and administrators are prohibited from being appointed. The rationale for excluding them is that having employees serve on the board could create a conflict of interest. While that may be an acceptable reason, why are no former faculty or retired academic administrators appointed to such bodies?

Unfortunately, knowledge of higher education does not appear to be an important criterion in the selection of board

Failed Grade

membership. Academicians on a board could probe academic priorities, how programs are initiated or terminated, examine the need for additional administrators and administrative travel expenses, and monitor budgets. Such information would contribute to the board's determining the effectiveness of senior administrators, terminate those who are failing, and rein in skyrocketing administrative salaries.[2] Instead, boards of trustees are emulating their industrial counterparts, but with one major difference: stockholders and quarterly financial reports provide the public with a degree of transparency for public companies that does not exist for colleges and universities.

Board's Role in Institutional Priorities

Priorities are no longer developed with great input from faculty, staff, and students. In the corporate culture, senior administrators make the decisions with the approval of boards of trustees serving largely as a "rubber stamp." In such an environment, decisions can be made more rapidly. But there is little justification for expediting important decisions. In such haste, college deans, department chairs, faculty, staff, and students now have less to say about institutional priorities and decisions. Presidents and provosts and their staffs have full authority and responsibility. This trend may have unforeseen consequences for higher education.

I'm not suggesting that all board members have no knowledge and are incompetent. On the contrary, I have seen some excellent people, who, despite lacking knowledge and preparation, take their board responsibilities

Boards of Trustees

very seriously. They educate themselves regarding the state of higher education and the institutions they are serving, in particular. However, these may be the exceptions rather than the rule. Most have limited understanding of higher education and do not understand what their roles should be with respect to overseeing senior administrators. In fact, their education comes largely from the very people they should be monitoring and advising.

Being a member on a college board has no financial remuneration. Therefore, attendance at board meetings can be highly variable and is based on the schedules of busy people serving as board members. For corporate executives, in particular, with many demands upon their time, attendance at university board meetings can be, at times, a lower priority.

Frequently, board members attend some of the social and athletic events of the institution, and they may participate in fundraising activities as well. In a sense, their involvement in the institution is often more ceremonial than substantive. Because board members typically function merely as an acquiescent body for the university administration, the success or failure of the institution rests solely on the president.

But relying only on a college president places an institution at great risk. The assumption that the president has excellent qualities and will serve the institution well is simply that—an assumption. If the individual has mediocre credentials and little vision for where his or her institution should be going, what then? It can be a prescription for disaster.

Failed Grade

Wallace Atwood, in 1921, became the first president when Clark College and Clark University were combined. Clark University, a small university in Massachusetts, had a few superb programs that were internationally recognized. Its program in psychology was sufficiently renowned that when Freud came to this country in the early 1900s, he chose this one institution as the place he wanted to lecture. Dr. Atwood, when he became president, built the Graduate School of Geography—an area of his expertise—but neglected all other programs. Quickly reading the focus of the new administration, the best faculty members in other disciplines departed and the institution went downhill, losing its reputation in everything but geography. It took many decades after this president left for the university to begin reestablishing the reputation it had once enjoyed in other areas. In effect, that president had succeeded in destroying many quality programs. Where was the board of trustees?

Reasons for Academicians on the Board

It is precisely for this reason a board of trustees should have some academicians in its ranks with a broad understanding of higher education, and a vision of where the institution should be heading. Even with the corporate model, these boards should have a major role in holding a university president accountable, since no one else in the institution can.

In its role, the board should focus on some key questions:

Boards of Trustees

- Is this senior administrator meeting the academic mission the board has established for the institution?
- How effective is he or she in enhancing academic quality, in recruiting and retaining superior associate administrators, faculty, staff, and students, and in improving the academic environment for everyone involved?
- Have the financial resources available been used prudently and cost-effectively?
- Has he or she been judicious in determining which programs survive and deserve more attention and which ones should be discontinued?
- Has he or she been effective in moderating tuition increases and encouraging access by the less affluent?
- How should the president be evaluated from the standpoint of total compensation, annual salary increments, and possible reappointment?

To be effective, a board of trustees must be capable of addressing these questions. In addition, it should be the responsibility of every board member to learn as much as he or she can about higher education and, more specifically, the institution they serve. Board members must take the initiative to learn about the best programs in the institution directly from the faculty, unit administrators, and the students involved. What factors have made them superior? How can that information be used to improve

Failed Grade

other programs? Though financial resources are important, they are less so than program leadership.

Students, faculty, and unit administrators are important constituencies and one can and should learn from them. To know academic quality, one must experience it firsthand and meet the people involved. Accepting a position on a board comes with ethical obligations as well as the responsibility for understanding the inner workings of the institution one serves.

To that end, appointments to boards of trustees should not be as payment for past services or for political purposes. Instead, individuals should be selected based on their backgrounds, their ability and desire to serve the institution, and a willingness to spend the time needed. Board positions have never been more important, given the corporate environment and the decreased involvement of faculty in decision making and institutional governance.

If institutions and/or governors continue appointing individuals with inadequate expertise, they may want to consider creating two boards: an honorary board, as currently constituted, and a second "operations" board charged with significant policy-making responsibility and oversight authority. The honorary board would still assist the president and other administrators with fundraising and attend graduation exercises and various social and athletic events. The latter would work with the president and other administrators in formulating academic policy, establishing budgets, making promotion and tenure decisions, and overseeing activities of the president and provost. Individuals serving on the operations board would be

54

Boards of Trustees

responsible for determining the total compensation and salaries for senior administrators.

To hold positions on the operations board, appointees would have to meet certain qualifications. Some of the individuals would be expected, through experience, to understand the inner workings of colleges and universities, either as former faculty or administrators. They must serve only on a single college board at a time to avoid potential conflicts of interest.

To recruit qualified individuals, it may be essential that such positions have financial compensation, not unlike corporate boards. Compensation should not be excessive, but sufficient to provide an incentive so board members take their responsibilities seriously, including attendance at regular board meetings.

The importance of board positions is shown as increasing numbers of college and university presidents are selected from among those who have been on university boards. Board positions apparently provide instant credibility. Politicians and business people have used such roles to further their careers. As an example, Hiram College, a small liberal arts college in Ohio, recently hired as its president a man who served as director of development for Cleveland's Gateway Sports Complex. He has no academic experience but had served on the college's board for 11 years.[3] Recent presidents at Florida State University and the University of Massachusetts have held important positions in their respective state legislatures. Serving on state boards of higher education now also requires no academic experience, and yet, as will be seen,

Failed Grade

the responsibility and the potential impact of such individuals on higher education in their states can be enormous.

Chapter Five
Boards of Regents or State Boards of Higher Education

Role of Boards of Regents

While boards of trustees have historically not been very proactive in monitoring the effectiveness of administrators in their institutions or even appreciating the direction of higher education nationally, it is the sole charge of the boards of regents, also known as state boards of higher education, to determine what are the higher educational needs of the state.[1] Their major role is to ensure access to all qualified students and to measure the quality of existing programs.

These boards have significant oversight responsibility guaranteeing that the education students receive in colleges and universities is a quality one and remains affordable and accessible to all types of students. The public cannot determine whether or not any educational program meets accepted national standards by simply examining brochures

Failed Grade

or visiting a campus; they depend on the boards of regents. Originally, such bodies were created as "ombudsmen" to provide an independent voice on higher educational issues reflecting society's best interests. Unfortunately, their role has become so modified that many have become political entities with virtually no independence from the political establishment. Elected officials with their own political agendas control them.

At one time, when the board in the state of Ohio had individuals with higher-education experience, they recommended that the number of medical schools be reduced from seven to four. Medical education is very expensive, and returning the number to what it had been previously, before three schools were added, would save a great deal of money. Those resources could be used for medical scholarships, increasing class size at those schools retained, and improving clinical education. But the state legislature was outraged at the recommendation and came within a single vote of abolishing the board of regents itself. Politicians viewed the issue not as an educational matter but for legislators to decide how many schools were needed and where they should be located. Needless to say, the state did not close any medical schools or eliminate state subsidy to those institutions.

In the past, members of the board had some academic expertise. The make-up of many is now composed of lawyers, business managers, and political operatives who, though serving in policymaking roles, have little knowledge of higher education. In a sense, board members chosen are beholden to the political establishment.

Boards of Regents or State Boards of Higher Education

An egregious example of the shenanigans of such a board occurred in Massachusetts. The Hampden School of Pharmacy, which opened in 1927, was never accredited by the national accrediting agency for pharmacy programs, the American Council on Pharmaceutical Education. Yet, the program was permitted to operate and enroll students until 1977, when it was acquired by the Massachusetts College of Pharmacy and Health Sciences, which had a nationally accredited pharmacy program.[2] Students who graduated from Hampden School of Pharmacy prior to 1977 were allowed to practice in Massachusetts, but nowhere else in the United States, since it was unaccredited and there was no reciprocity with other states.

It's unlikely that many students knew when they enrolled that their education would be substandard and they would be limited as to where they could practice. Also, patients using the pharmaceutical services of such graduates were unaware these health providers had been trained in a program that was not nationally accredited. Why would such a program be permitted to function?

A senior political leader in the state legislature and the owner of the school were close personal friends, and there was no way the political leader would prevent graduates from the program from practicing in the state. In effect, the state board ignored the school's lack of accreditation. Politics was more important than academic quality, to the detriment of all.

A less egregious example, but one that may be more pernicious in the long run, has been the proliferation of four-year colleges and health science programs in a number

Failed Grade

of states. The rationale for creating these programs has been that students should be able to gain a college education within a reasonable distance from where they live. On the face of it, this sounds rational. But the real reason programs are multiplying is politicians want to be perceived as doing something for their constituents. One way has been to establish colleges and universities in the districts they serve, despite the fact that many students are willing to take out loans and travel significant distances to go to prestigious universities, if they are admitted.

An example of how the political process bypassed the board of regents is illustrated by an incident in Ohio. Prior to July 1986 Shawnee State Community College had twenty-seven academic majors in which all were one-year certificate or associate degree programs. But the speaker of the Ohio House of Representatives decided he wanted to convert this school to primarily baccalaureate degree programs. He authored legislation that passed in the house, then the senate, and was signed into law by the governor, making the college Shawnee State University in 1986. Is there anything wrong with such a development? Aren't more educational opportunities desirable? How could one say no? But the board of regents had been effectively bypassed with no justification that an additional state university was needed, especially if standards might have to be lowered. More critically, during economic downturns when the state budget for all colleges and universities is reduced, an additional state university becomes a burden that contributes ultimately to increased tuition for all students.

60

Boards of Regents or State Boards of Higher Education

The continued proliferation of colleges within states is comparable to "pork barrel" legislation at the federal level. After all, new colleges and universities create construction jobs and contracts, which are incestuously tied to the political establishment. In the above example, Shawnee State had seven buildings in 1986; it had twenty-four in 1999.

Even during poor economic times, construction thrives at state colleges and universities while operating budgets are being slashed and educational standards are eroded. New buildings are viewed as a job creation project, so they must be continued. Also new institutions infuse money into the local economy through recruiting of faculty and staff and purchase of goods and services by students, faculty, and staff. Formation of new schools usually occurs during times of economic prosperity when tax revenues are high, and since new taxes are not required to initiate new institutions, the public doesn't pay any attention. Bond issues for construction costs provide a painless mechanism by which payments are deferred to future taxpayers.

Optimal Use of the Higher-Education Budget

There are a number of solutions to the problem of college, university, and program proliferation, but implicit in all of these is the key responsibility of the board to make decisions that are academically, not politically, driven. The board must ensure that the budget for higher education is optimally used. For instance, if additional graduates were needed in a particular discipline, one alternative would be to expand existing programs. The cost of this option is

Failed Grade

considerably less than forming a new institution or program, and students would be enrolled in programs with established quality.

When inevitable economic downturns occur, one of the first budgets governors and state legislatures slash is higher education. Politicians find this more palatable than raising taxes since the higher-education lobby, consisting largely of students, their families, and the employees of these institutions, has considerably less clout than other constituencies. Invariably, education cuts tend to go across the board, and programs ranging from the mediocre to excellent are all adversely affected.

In the corporate sector, when companies experience a decline in revenue, under-performing and costly programs, as well as marginal employees, are terminated. This process is known as "downsizing," which is followed by "restructuring." There are no across-the-board reductions in corporations. Effective programs and projects are maintained and supported since they will be the basis by which the company survives and expands in the future.

But as yet, no such restructuring mechanisms are used for institutions of higher education. It is the one area of the corporate sector that should be applied to higher education and is only now being proposed.[3] The problem for state institutions is the question of what can be done with tenured faculty and civil servants. The board must be both sensitive to the problem of people and also propose creative solutions.

I am not proposing sweeping closures of different academic programs or various institutions based only on

Boards of Regents or State Boards of Higher Education

short-term economic conditions, since downturns have proved to be only temporary. However, state boards of higher education should play a major role at such times in developing contingency plans and examining how the health of higher education can be maintained and improved through downsizing and restructuring.

Times of economic stress should provide the opportunity and impetus for institutions to reexamine their programs, determining which are good and which are marginal. And, the board of higher education should assist and encourage colleges and universities through restructuring costs to terminate marginal programs; especially if one-time-only expenses are involved. Though it certainly may be desirable to have multiple state-supported and private programs for meeting community needs, the ultimate litmus test should be: "Which of these programs merit retention and which do not?" With declining tax revenues, maximizing the use of state revenues in higher education should be an important priority. At times, state boards have questioned the need for certain graduate programs, especially in institutions where there are only one or two students enrolled. And yet, many boards have been ineffective in ending even such marginal programs.

The Board in Inter-institutional Corporation

In order to assist schools, there should be some degree of inter-institutional restructuring—an area where the board's involvement would be vital. Coalescing weak programs into strong ones may be a way of both closing marginal programs and improving existing programs. Finally, a

63

Failed Grade

board needs to have the ability to assist colleges by moving a program from one publicly funded institution to another. In South Carolina, the pharmacy programs at the University of South Carolina at Columbia and at the Medical College of South Carolina in Charleston are being merged. The state's shortfall in revenues is providing the impetus.

This may be a radical concept, eliciting strong objections from the institution from which a program is removed, as well as from politicians in that district. But if the alternative is no state support will be provided for students enrolled in certain programs, institutions are likely to acquiesce; especially if the rationale makes good educational and financial sense. If the state must further trim its financial support, this can be accomplished by reducing the number of new students enrolling in existing programs.

The transfer of faculty and staff from one institution to another might be traumatic but should be considered a viable option. Students already in the program must not be disadvantaged; also that is the reason for a long time horizon in carrying out changes. Obviously, such decisions should only occur after careful deliberation by the board, the agreement of unbiased experts, and ultimately the approval of affected institutions. At the heart of the matter should be the responsibility of the board to maximize the use of state funds.

Colleges and universities can assist by reducing administrative costs in times of economic constraint, but boards should not micromanage state institutions. Since state funds are provided to support student enrollment, boards of higher education have crucial responsibility in

Boards of Regents or State Boards of Higher Education

ensuring quality of education is not compromised during economic contractions. Students and their families have a right to assume state colleges and universities are continually being monitored in this regard. Where state boards keep institutions open for political and not academic reasons, valuable tax and student dollars are squandered unnecessarily.

The Board's Role in Unmet Academic Needs and Access

In addition to recommending the closure or merger of existing programs, another board function is identifying unmet academic needs. It may encourage various institutions, either publicly or privately funded, to establish a new program unavailable in the state for which there is a need. An important requirement for creating a new program is an institution is interested and possesses the necessary facilities, financial support, and academic expertise in the specific discipline being added.

Finally, it is important for the board to address the issue of access and student retention. While it may not be the board's role to determine levels of state subsidy provided to colleges and universities nor address the tuition at state-supported institutions, the board could nevertheless examine factors contributing to escalating tuition rates. For instance, are skyrocketing costs due to un-funded mandates from the state and federal governments? Do excessive administrative costs contribute to tuition increases? What can the board do to reduce high tuition costs by working

Failed Grade

with various institutional constituencies and the political establishment?

Remedial Education

Another area contributing to increasing costs is remedial education. When colleges and universities provide remedial education to students whose primary and secondary education was inadequate, significant costs are involved. In the State of Ohio, 38 percent of those enrolled in state public colleges took remedial classes.[4] Higher education should not bear the costs for students who arrive unprepared to handle college-level courses. The board of regents should strongly discourage acceptance of these individuals into four-year colleges and universities. Rather, the financial burden for these students should lie with primary and secondary schools, community colleges, and the students themselves. Otherwise, resources in the higher-education budget are being wasted.

Expertise of Board Members

Given the responsibility placed on state boards, it is apparent why members of the board of regents must have some expertise on how colleges and universities function. For this reason, a majority of its members should be academicians possessing the necessary qualifications and must have some degree of independence from the political establishment. Otherwise, it becomes impossible to end remedial education, close marginal institutions, or suggest the combination of programs that have political sponsorship.

Boards of Regents or State Boards of Higher Education

Colleges and universities are beginning to resemble military bases at the federal level. Once institutions are started, they are difficult to close—even if performing marginally and not serving students, society, and the taxpayers. Such restructuring options are clearly necessary, especially with the economic roller coaster most state-supported colleges have ridden. The question is not whether the board of regents should be insulated from political machinations, but how they can operate effectively within the system. Perhaps if board members were elected officials, they might feel more accountability to their constituents; however, this process would likely have its own pitfalls. So, if it is impossible for the board of regents to have some political independence, perhaps it should be eliminated. Staff personnel who are responsible to the governor and/or state legislature could handle its functions. The cost savings recognized by eliminating boards could be used for student scholarships and other educational initiatives.

This solution is not optimal because the board of regents has very important functions that no other organization in the state can provide. Ironically, they were created to insulate higher education from the demands of the political establishment. But without some modicum of political independence, there is little they can accomplish. And if they can't effectively serve the interests of the people of the state, then why retain them? Perhaps the solution lies in giving all of the responsibility back to the politicians, who are driving the process and controlling the

67

Failed Grade

funds anyway. Then, failure resides at their doorstep, and they must accept the full consequences.

Chapter Six
Faculty and Tenure Matters

The Importance of Senior Faculty

Faculty members are the key personnel of any college or university. I say this not as a retired faculty member, but as a former academic administrator. Professors are the interface between the institution and the students. Together with the students and the administration, faculty members create the institution's esprit de corps and foster the environment for learning. Faculties determine what should be taught, based on the institution's or program's established curriculum. Faculty must not only ensure material provided for students is current but also look ahead to what future graduates will need to be successful. The faculty's responsibility includes designing examinations and assigning papers and readings to measure whether students have mastered a particular subject and

Failed Grade

whether they can apply the acquired knowledge satisfactorily. It is a tall order.

The quality of an institution's faculty correlates with the quality of education delivered. Therefore, it is imperative for administrators and senior faculty to attract the best and brightest colleagues, and importantly, to retain them. Without good faculty, an institution has a mediocre educational environment.

In my view, the main role of colleges and universities is educating the next generation of students. Everything else should be secondary to that objective. Therefore faculty recruitment is an institution's highest priority. Administrators come and go, but top-notch faculty members are the basis for an institution's teaching and scholarly success. Many students recognize what faculty members help them accomplish. They appreciate the many hours faculty spend advising them, preparing lectures and laboratory experiments and developing fair examinations. Some former students express appreciation by donating financially, in the form of scholarships, research funding, and endowed chairs. And, in some cases, these gifts are given in the name of a specific faculty member.

Some administrators fail to appreciate what superior, senior faculty members do for an institution. When told that three hundred senior faculty members opted for early retirement, one provost commented that nothing unusual had happened and that students in the autumn quarter would be unaware of what had occurred. That was an outrageous comment! If he meant classes would still be held, he was correct. But if he was inferring that the quality

70

Faculty and Tenure Matters

of education would be unaltered, he couldn't have been further from the truth. Implying that the departure of so many senior people with significant teaching experience would have little effect on the academic environment is ludicrous.

The Importance of Tenure

It is precisely for this reason that tenure is so important. Tenure is simply the process by which institutions determine whether a particular faculty member will be offered a permanent teaching position. Typically, a faculty member beginning an academic career applies for tenure after five to seven years of teaching at an institution.[1] That time frame can be shorter for those who arrive with greater experience, or longer for those in clinical positions.

This concept of permanent employment is not confined to faculty positions in colleges and universities. It applies to teaching positions in primary and secondary schools, to judges in various courts, and to those in civil service positions in state and federal government. There will always be cases of abuse; but in general, the tenure system works well because it fosters commitment of the individual to the institution he or she serves.

The period leading to tenure is considered "probationary." It permits administrators and senior faculty colleagues to determine whether junior members have the teaching and scholarly potential to make a strong and continuing contribution to a department's academic program. A tenure decision has long-term implications for the institution, the academic program, students and

Failed Grade

potential faculty colleagues. For this reason, tenure decisions are not taken lightly. If an institution harbors doubts about granting tenure, it should err on the side of denying it. It is preferable to lose someone who might have potential, rather than award tenure to an individual who may be wrong in the long term. Those not awarded tenure at one institution might gain it at another. I have certainly known cases where that has occurred. Perhaps they may have learned from past mistakes and applied themselves more effectively at another institution.

For people considering an academic career, the security offered by tenure is an important consideration. After all, if there is no security for a new faculty member, there may be little incentive to teach effectively and become part of that institution. Lack of job security can be an obstacle in attracting and retaining the most qualified people, ultimately affecting the long-term success of an institution. The value of tenure is that it adds security to the position and may prevent scholars from opting to join the private business sector, where the financial rewards are greater.

Two critical issues adversely affecting faculty members today are eliminating tenure and university governance. Tenure is under attack from many factions, including administrators,[2] business and political types,[3] the media,[4] and even faculty members themselves as stated by Bercuson, Bothwell and Granatstein.[5] They say, "The only answer, therefore, is limited-term, renewable contracts. The good faculty—the competent researchers and the effective teachers—will have no trouble continuing their careers successfully under this regime. With luck and some

Faculty and Tenure Matters

administrative courage, the dead-wood, no longer protected by job-security tenure, will be pruned at last."

The argument for ending tenure and substituting "term appointments" revolves around the issue that some faculty members, granted tenure early in their careers, become unproductive later and are no longer dynamic and effective as they once were. It is a valid dilemma that should be addressed.

In my own experiences, I've observed few cases of nonfunctioning tenured faculty that merited termination. The time to identify and eliminate marginal people should be during the probationary period. In most instances, this period is used for that purpose. The large majority of tenured faculty members want to contribute positively to their institution. And concerned administrators with a vested interest in seeing tenured faculty succeed can usually help those who have become less effective as a teacher or scholar over time.

There seems to be little reason therefore to dismantle a system that has worked effectively for hundreds of years in colleges and universities. As Henry Rosovsky states,[6] "Let me now try to state the affirmative case for tenure as one of the necessary virtues of academic life. The first habitual line of defense is tenure as the principal guarantor of academic freedom."

Even those with serious reservations [7] admit the alternatives could be worse. We have little assurance that any alternative will be better or more effective. In fact, changes could have unexpected consequences that are far worse than the system it was designed to cure. We could

73

Failed Grade

witness the more rapid turnover of the best faculty looking for higher salaries, longer-term contracts, and greater security. Students would suffer from such mobility since the best faculty would have greater opportunity to get other positions in academia or industry.

One aspect of tenure rarely mentioned is that tenured faculty enter the permanent ranks of the institution's "family." This relationship implies not only a responsibility of the institution to the faculty member, but also a reciprocal commitment on the part of faculty to the institution—a two-way street, of sorts. With such loyalty, both the faculty member and the institution benefit.

An example of how an administrator can help a tenured faculty member and the institution involved my predecessor in the College of Pharmacy at The Ohio State University. He realized one of the faculty members was no longer effectively mentoring graduate students. However, the faculty member had, over the years, been an effective member of the college's community. Realizing the quandary existing for both this faculty member and the institution, the administrator offered him the opportunity to become part of the administration and assist faculty in undergraduate course planning, working with students individually so they would complete their pharmacy program in a timely fashion. The faculty member knew the program very well, and there was a clear need for a person with his background and expertise.

This particular faculty member accepted the new challenge. He was a hardworking person and did an admirable job in this new position. Both faculty and

Faculty and Tenure Matters

students respected him for what he was able to accomplish for each group. When he ultimately retired, there was an outpouring of goodwill from former students around the country. Three staff people were required to replace him. In short, because he was part of the "family," he approached his responsibility to the institution seriously.

The challenge for administrators is to maximize the contributions of the various faculty members they supervise. Administrators have some responsibility when a faculty member fails to work at his optimum potential. Attentive and competent administrators should pick up signals early when a person becomes less productive. They can assist floundering colleagues and coach them to improve performance instead of ignoring them.

In another instance, a faculty member's research skills were no longer at the cutting edge. The dean realized these needed to be refurbished. He encouraged the faculty member to take a sabbatical year at an excellent university. When he returned, his research career was reborn. He remained productive until he retired.

The attack on tenure is composed of two parts: (1) the elimination of so-called "dead wood" by termination of unproductive tenured faculty and (2) administrators' desires to control the downstream costs of their programs. Both have merit, but in the corporate culture, the latter is of more critical importance. Replacing senior, more expensive, faculty with junior or part-time ones offers a college an important financial incentive. And from a corporate viewpoint, fiscal policy is a paramount issue. To assess the

75

Failed Grade

value of tenure, it is useful to examine the conditions in institutions without tenure.

A Non-tenured Environment

Instead of tenure, there has been discussion of giving faculty "fixed-term" appointments of four or five years. Faculty in such an environment would not look upon themselves as a permanent part of the institution. It could create the feeling of "every man for himself," where entrepreneurship reigns supreme.

Then, too, some of the better and more dynamic people could become actively involved in looking for new, more secure, and better-paying positions early in their terms. An atmosphere of increased mobility for faculty would prevail to the detriment of both the academic program and the students. No loyalty from the institution would engender a similar lack of commitment from the faculty. But even if those conditions were not to occur, faculty would feel vulnerable to the vagaries of administrators all the time and not just during the probationary period. The way groups of people address vulnerability is to organize. That has already occurred at some universities, such as the University of Cincinnati and Temple University.

If tenure were to end, it's likely that more faculty would choose to organize, thereby creating a union versus management environment. Unionization is generally the response to administrative ineptitude. In fact, in colleges where it has occurred, there is an adversarial relationship between faculty and administration, and this tension in turn

Faculty and Tenure Matters

adversely affects the learning environment for students, which is not readily reversed.

In a union environment, negotiations between faculty and institutions would no longer be limited to salaries but would likely include working conditions as well, ranging from faculty involvement in student advising to faculty roles in student and professional organizations and committee activities. As often happens in union environments, faculty would likely begin to feel they were merely "hired hands," no longer a permanent part of the institution's family and begin to act as such. Every decision affecting the faculty would require negotiation and be decided through a third party and collective bargaining. The easy rapport between faculty and administration found in a collegial environment would be a thing of the past.

So the real issue is not whether we should replace tenure with term appointments, but whether to eliminate tenure and face unionization.[8] As a former administrator, I would prefer working within a tenure system rather than deal with a unionized faculty. Before eliminating tenure, the consequences of doing so need to be carefully evaluated.

Faculty Governance

The second big area under attack in the corporate world of academia is faculty governance. What is governance? Here's how one administrator, Henry Rosovsky, Dean of the Faculty of Arts and Sciences from 1973 to 1984 and Acting President of Harvard University in 1984 and 1987, author of *The University: An Owner's Manual*, described it: "Governance concerns power: who is in charge; who makes

Failed Grade

decisions; who has a voice, and how loud is that voice? These are always complicated and contentious questions especially in higher education."[9]

Frank H. T. Rhodes, president emeritus at Cornell, argues in his book[10] that faculty involvement in institutional governance is outmoded, "inflexible and ponderous in an age that requires institutions to be nimble and adaptive" and that the success of universities in the future will rest on the ability to complement the best features of faculty governance with "more creative engagement by the governing board and more decisive presidential leadership." Certainly, it is easier and faster for administrators to make decisions in the corporate mode without the need for faculty consensus. With all of the issues put before an administrative staff, it is easy to understand the temptation to act fast. Being nimble, however, is not nearly as critical as making the best decision for the institution and having it widely accepted. After all, universities are generally not competing with other institutions and under time pressures as corporations.

Faculty involvement in governance ensures that administrators must justify their actions and don't have carte blanche in decision making. Faculty satisfaction is very important to ensuring that turnover is minimized, especially among the best faculty. The "top-down" corporate decision making permeating many institutions today threatens the partnership between administrators and faculty and the academic family concept which has been instrumental in creating a good learning environment for students for many decades.

Chapter Seven
Students and Their Expectations

Career Decisions

Probably the first important decision a senior in high school makes is whether or not to go to college. Attending college has significant economic benefits over those who terminate their education at high school. Therefore, many plan a college education for financial reasons.[1] Then the question is which college to apply to and is there reasonable expectation one would be accepted?

For many, making this decision appears a daunting task. The differentiation of secondary schools into college preparatory, commercial, and trade schools has long since disappeared. Education is no longer viewed as an end in itself, but as a means to an economic objective. And so, many students now go to college, even those with marginal abilities, groping with what they will do after graduation. Unclear career objectives apply not only to marginal students but to good ones as well.

Failed Grade

Students worry whether a career decision is the correct one, and is it irrevocable? Usually conclusions are arrived at with incomplete information. Fortunately for many, there is not just one college or a single career that is the only appropriate one. Nevertheless, there are careers that are inappropriate for some. How these can be sorted out is a problem facing many.

Unfortunately, high school has become a wasteland, and many guidance counselors are ineffective in helping students determine strengths and weaknesses and thereby possible careers. One can't make such an important decision by courses alone, because that may be a reflection of the effectiveness of the teacher in a particular discipline and one's relationship with that teacher. However, what can be decided in high school is whether to pursue a career requiring either a background in mathematics and the sciences or in business, arts, and the humanities.

Such a decision allows the student to choose the type of college and the initial program to enter. Narrowing down that choice can be difficult, especially for the better students. However, it is a beginning, and eliminating choices is frequently easier than making a positive career selection.

College itself should be an important time for exploring various options. As one might expect, student attitudes and expectations are variable and dependent upon family views, friends, and their socioeconomic status. Those in a lower socioeconomic status know at the outset that they don't have the luxury of deliberating too long. They must arrive at decisions early because they don't have the financial

Students and Their Expectations

resources to be an academic dilettante, transferring from one program to another.

For the affluent, the financial pressures may not be of major concern. But even these students know their decision cannot be open-ended. The fear of making the wrong decision can immobilize a student, thinking it is better to procrastinate than make a mistake. But both are decisions. The key question is whether a choice can be made without practical experience?

Yet in most colleges, there is little opportunity for students to have such exposure before making a decision. In essence, they muddle through with incomplete information. They discuss career options with classmates who are as inexperienced as they. Sometimes they talk with family members possessing little background. Rarely do students approach faculty members or outside professionals with their queries. When I was a faculty member and dean, few students asked my help in exploring various options open to them. That frequently occurred only when failure was looming on the horizon.

In one case, a student was failing our pharmacy program. He repetitively had great difficulty with the science courses. And finally, a faculty committee was prepared to dismiss him from the program. Before that occurred, I met with him inquiring why this career track was important to him. His uncle was a pharmacist, and he wanted to complete the program to be able to work with him. That was understandable, but he really lacked the academic skills.

Failed Grade

I asked him what courses he liked, those which came easy to him, and what practical experiences he had enjoyed. He had done well in the business courses and enjoyed them very much. He liked working in his uncle's pharmacy and viewed pharmacy more as a business than a profession. I encouraged his transfer to the business school and one of its programs. He did very well there, achieving a B average at the time of graduation. He subsequently became a successful stockbroker in the community and expressed his satisfaction with the business program and the guidance I had provided.

Students should possess good academic skills in programs they undertake and be willing to work hard to master the concepts. At least this indicates the subject matter is of interest and they possess ability. And while not the only yardstick, it is an important beginning that must be supplemented by practical experience in the field. One should try always to feed into one's strengths, not one's weaknesses.

Student Attitudes

Education is hard work. It does not come easily for most, even when the subject matter is interesting. Unfortunately, most students have been imbued with the notion from elementary schools that education should be fun and always enjoyable. Many have the idea that mastering material should come easily and not require hard work.

That is an unfortunate misconception of what education is. Many feel if they are not disruptive and are pleasant,

Students and Their Expectations

they are entitled to complete any program leading to a degree or a professional license. They view this as a right, whether or not they have ability or have demonstrated that academically.

One student I knew failed some essential science courses. She was placed multiple times on probation and finally dismissed from the program by a college committee. I informed her of the college's action. She responded she would continue appealing her dismissal until it was reversed. She was simply unwilling to accept academic standards and felt persistence would force a change. She was wrong. But this illustrates a consumer mentality with which academic institutions must cope.

Her attitude was created in part by the political environment. This same political establishment is wringing its proverbial hands at the sorry state of primary and secondary education today. A recent incidence of plagiarism in high school by students in a biology class resulted in the teacher failing 20 percent of the students. Her decision was supported by the principal and by the superintendent, but the school board, after complaints from parents, ordered the teacher to reverse her decision. The teacher resigned, but the result of the school board's action was not lost on the students.

Any decision can be reversed, regardless of academic or ethical justification. Pressure and persistence is all that is required. Another relevant example I cite occurred when I was teaching a graduate course in biochemistry. It was offered in the evening to permit students who had full-time jobs to take this course at a more convenient time. On one

Failed Grade

occasion after the course was over, a student came to see me. He told me he had received a failing grade and in reviewing his records, I concurred.

He asked what he could do to receive a passing grade. I told him he could repeat the course. He told me that was not why he came to see me and asked whether he could take another exam. I told him if he had that opportunity, anyone else should be afforded the same recourse.

He countered asking whether he could do a report for extra credit and thereby pass the course. I responded, as previously, that such an opportunity should be given everyone. But, he said that others have not made that request. I replied that it would be unfair if he were treated in a special way without providing that opportunity to anyone else.

He finally concluded, "You mean I failed the course?" I said, "Yes." He told me he taught chemistry in high school and they didn't do it that way. I retorted that was the problem.

In attempting to shield children from failure, we are preparing them for even greater disappointments in the future. I've learned more from my failures than successes. Education should be preparatory for real-life experiences, and the responsibility for a student's education must rest squarely on the student's shoulders. As Dr. Rhodes in quoting Andrew D. White, the first president of Cornell University, a century ago said,[2] "You are not here to receive an education. You are here to educate yourselves."

Students should not be deluded into feeling they will always succeed even if they haven't worked hard to meet

Students and Their Expectations

objectives. Such delusions can have tragic future consequences for them, as described by Professor Perlmutter of Louisiana State University in his article entitled, "Going to college? Here's how to fail."[3] He says, "Some of the surefire ways to fail:

- Don't develop any short- or long-term professional goals.
- Think of education as a chore, not a tool.
- Don't spend time with good students.
- Don't manage your time wisely.
- Don't ask for help."

Some current attitudes are creating a generation with supreme but unwarranted confidence. One consequence is a willingness to challenge professors and administrators regarding grades, courses, prerequisites, and the composition of programs. Some students even feel they know what material they'll need when they finish their programs and question why they must take certain courses. They fail to realize such issues have been debated numerous times by the faculty. This arrogance derives from a lack of knowledge. A quote by Mark Twain is relevant where one could replace father with professor: "When I was...fourteen, my father was so ignorant I could hardly stand to have the old man around. But when I got to be twenty-one, I was astonished at how much he had learned in seven years."

A legacy of the Vietnam era was the right to challenge authority because of the failures of the political establishment at that time. This mentality persists today in many facets of society whether justified or not. And it

Failed Grade

occurs by individuals with little understanding as to how academic programs are developed, the rationale for courses, and their sequence in a program. Such unwarranted confidence is enhanced by selecting students to be members of boards of trustees at colleges and universities and even by requesting their input in "Student Evaluation of Teaching" forms. While student input is certainly desirable, peer input may be more useful since these are professionals with greater experience.

Another factor affecting many students is their interest in establishing close and intense personal relationships with other individuals of the opposite or same sex. Such distractions are occurring earlier in a person's life, when students are in college and away from home. These are not usually lifetime commitments, but their intensity and preoccupation can be a serious distraction from focusing on education and the need to determine a career.

College Education as a Part-Time Activity

Another serious distraction is the need or desire of students to obtain part-time or even full-time work. For those with the burden of paying for their own education, this requirement is a necessity, especially with the increasing costs of college education. Still others may want financial resources for cars, off-campus living, vacations, and entertainment that their parents are unable or unwilling to provide.

Postponed gratification isn't in the lexicon of many college students today. This problem of coping with increasing numbers of students working many hours off

Students and Their Expectations

campus is a serious one. The competition between work and study is real. And as a consequence, we are seeing more students extending time of graduation from four years to five and even beyond.

I was involved in teaching a course whose purpose was to show various professional opportunities and careers for students after completing their pharmacy program. Professionals were brought in as guest lecturers for topics illustrating the background needed for a particular career. It was a valuable exposure for all students in the program and was a required course.

One student complained to me that since the course was offered at 8:00 A.M., it was very inconvenient for him to come. He was working in the evening at a part-time job and had difficulty getting up early. He asked whether it was necessary for him to come. I was surprised at his audacity. Clearly, his part-time job was more important than his education, and indirectly he was questioning the relevance of the required course. Students often attempt to schedule classes to mesh with their work and not vice-a-versa.

Education is one area where many are not interested in getting their money's worth. When purchasing a house, car, or television, they want the best value obtainable for the money. But in education, the objective seems for some to do the least work possible to obtain a degree. By work, I am, of course, referring to studying, not working for pay.

I'll cite one example. At the end of a professional science course, I examined the grades of those who had failed. I was never happy with failures even if there were few. Advanced students should pass if they had applied

Failed Grade

themselves. I never failed a certain percentage because that would be unfair to students. Yet, I was unprepared to lower standards.

When reviewing these final grades, I noticed no grades for the unannounced quizzes of one failing student. I called asking if I had made an error in not recording her quiz grades. She told me she failed the course the previous year and had not attended classes when the quizzes were given because she was working. It reminds me what Thomas Huxley once said, "Perhaps the most valuable result of all education is the ability to make yourself do the thing you have to do, when it ought to be done and whether you like it or not; it is the first lesson to be learned; and however early a man's training begins, it is probably the last lesson that he learns thoroughly."

Mine was a marginal student who did not learn this lesson. I was nonplussed at her irresponsibility. I hadn't failed her: she had earned her failure.

The idea that education is part-time never ceases to amaze me. When completing my undergraduate degree in chemistry at an engineering school, there were full days of classes and laboratories from Monday through Friday with the exception of one free afternoon. Classes on Saturday were from 8:00 A.M. through 12:00 noon. It was impossible for any student to have even a part-time job. Yet all students, who successfully finished, did so in four years; that was the expectations at that time.

Students and Their Expectations

Social Promotion and Consumerism in College

In addition, students have begun to expect social promotion in higher education. They view themselves as paying "customers," consumers if you will. Zachary Karabell has said it very well[4]: "Entering the university with the attitude of consumers, students grade their classes and their professors on student evaluations much as *Consumer Reports* rates dishwashers. Deans and administrators, competing for students in a competitive market, respond to student and parental whims, and educational standards are the casualty."

Students feel if they pay the tuition, they are entitled to complete any program. They are frustrated when faculty and administrators insist that academic prerequisites and standards be met. That has not been their prior educational experience.

The concept of students as "customers" was probably first proposed by Peter Drucker in his book entitled, *The Effective Executive*[5] when he wrote (p.60-61) "Perhaps the greatest shortcoming of the present generation of university presidents in the United States is their inside focus on administration, on money-raising, and so on. Yet no other administrator in the large university is free to establish contact with students who are the university's 'customers.'" When President of The Ohio State University E. Gordon Gee supported this argument, he was quoted in the campus newspaper, *Ohio State Lantern,*[6] when talking about students, "...the university and the customers it serves." "Quality is the ultimate issue for the university and the

89

Failed Grade

customers it serves," Gee said, referring to faculty, students, their parents, and alumni.

The concept of students as "customers" is a clearly misguided one. One wouldn't call patients of physicians or clients of lawyers, "customers." Similarly, students aren't customers. They come to the university to be educated by professionals who should decide what knowledge they need to complete their program. To do otherwise, the curriculum becomes a giant smorgasbord, decided by neophytes. But in this consumer age, the "customer" is always right, and how can anyone fail a "customer"?

A few years ago, I was involved in a foreign country with a team responsible for evaluating a health-science program. When the administrator in charge was asked the percentage of entering students who had failed, he was nonplussed. He said the academic quality of the students was very high, that only 10 to 15 percent of applicants were admitted. But since every student admitted was almost guaranteed a degree, a climate had been created with little incentive for students to work hard and learn as much as possible.

In essence, too much security had become a de-motivating environment for learning. Arbitrarily failing a percentage of students is grossly unfair, but passing all regardless of performance is wrong both for those who apply themselves and for those who do not. The former are perceived as being foolish since all will receive the same degree regardless of performance. The better students in that program confirmed the view that too much security was a corrosive influence. A humorous statement comes to

Students and Their Expectations

mind: "What do you call the person who finishes last in his medical class? Why you call him or her 'Doctor'."

In yet another country, it was difficult for students to be accepted into the more prestigious universities. They worked very hard in primary and secondary schools to compete in countrywide examinations that determined their future institutions. It was a stressful time. However, once enrolled in college, students were guaranteed a diploma since academic expectations were very modest. In effect, this also was social promotion and future careers were determined by the reputation of the university and not by the student's performance.

These arguments are used involving health professional programs at some Ivy League schools.[7] Since only high-quality students are enrolled, no one should fail. But the reasoning is fallacious since the student's brilliance is no gauge of academic performance. In the final analysis, the classroom and requisite examinations, unpleasant and stressful as these may be, create a more stimulating environment for all. It remains to be determined how decreasing institutional expectations of students and lowered academic standards affect preparation for careers in the corporate and professional worlds.

Higher education has been the crown jewel of the educational system in the United States, acting as a beacon for young people around the world. Scientific facilities are without peer. Foreign students who come realize they must work hard in order to achieve since English is usually not their native language. For them, education is hard work and not a part-time endeavor in which courses are merely

Failed Grade

interspersed between intense personal relationships and outside work requirements. Their diligence infuses the system and is beneficial for everyone, including those who are native born.

While American students now have a more complex social environment than earlier generations, even so, their education must not be shortchanged. It must have primacy for them, even with the competing demands. It is essential that they be adequately prepared for the world of tomorrow since the future will be a more complicated time with many career options available.

For this reason, students must use their college education to its fullest. It should not be viewed as merely a means to getting a high-paying job. No one knows with certainty what one will ultimately be doing in a complete professional life. Therefore, education is important for preparing one for the future, not merely an obstacle course.

Chapter Eight
Education versus Indoctrination. How Social and Political Agendas Discourage Independent Thinking

The corporate culture in our institutions has spawned an environment where many courses are offered based on popularity rather than academic rigor. As in the advertising industry, the number of viewers is an important criterion, and courses are offered if the number of students enrolling is high, since it is all about the financial imperative. This is a mistaken notion for many people wish to get the best education they can afford. They will take challenging courses and programs that will prepare them for a superior career and an enjoyable future life.

Failed Grade

Courses in a Program

In the past, courses offered were part of an entire program. There was a greater concern by the institution with a student's complete education; academic rigor increased as the student progressed through the program. This concept was considered important as the student mastered and then applied what had been learned. Perhaps that was a legacy of the environment in which students were seen as immature and the institution acted in loco parentis.

In the past, too, there was a rationale for required courses and the sequence in which these were offered. Whether that same rationale would apply today is not relevant, but there was an inherent consistency to the program. And the faculty and administration together devoted a great deal of time in program development. There was little concern regarding course popularity, and such issues weren't even on the radar screen.

Programs and courses were built upon prerequisites. Students were not allowed to enter a class for which they had not passed the required prerequisites. However on assuming my first major administrative position, I was appalled to find a student taking a required sophomore course in her senior year though it was a prerequisite for the rest of her program. She had failed the course on several occasions and yet had been allowed to take advanced courses for which the failed course was a prerequisite! Then in her senior year, she had to obtain a

Education versus Indoctrination

passing grade in the required sophomore course in order to graduate.

No one had been monitoring her progress in the program; there is a big difference between taking a prerequisite and successfully passing it. Either the course should not have been a prerequisite, but if it were, then mastering that material should have been relevant in subsequent courses. In an environment with no prerequisites, there is no such thing as a well-conceived program; the course of study is merely a collection of courses to be taken at the whim of the student.

Previously, it was unheard of for students to feign ignorance of the subject matter in a prerequisite. Many do that now, as if they have a short attention span or possess academic amnesia. Implicit is the comment of some, "I passed that course and promptly forgot it, so don't expect me to remember anything that was taught in it."

Now, time must often be spent in a new class refreshing student knowledge included in the prerequisite. It is a form of remedial education or "dumbing down" that occurs all the time now in colleges and universities. According to Zachary Karabell in *What's College For? The Struggle to Define American Higher* Education,[1] "This 'dumbing down' is particularly prevalent in the humanities, where the courses are harder to justify to students and parents, both of whom view college almost entirely in job-oriented terms." College is viewed as preparation for a job only, says Karabell;[2] "Job concerns occupy all college students from the most elite to those at the most down-at-the-heels community college." Such an attitude is exacerbated when

95

Failed Grade

Karabell states[3] "As the United States enters the twenty-first century, a quiet revolution is occurring: Higher education is becoming mass education and the process is being radically democratized." Students do not view education as promoting intellectual growth; rather there is only one reason to go to college—getting a good-paying job.

Entertainment vs Education

Many students now want their pleasure centers stimulated rather than to be challenged intellectually. This is not a brief against entertaining faculty or popular courses. But the purpose of a college education should be to help students grow intellectually, providing the bedrock upon which further growth will occur in their personal and professional lives. I strongly support the view enunciated by Robert and Jon Solomon[4] in *Up the University—Recreating Higher Education in America* when they say, "Our main theme, which will outrage many educators, is that the primary business of the university is education." And further, as they state,[5] "As we have said, the entire process of higher education should be aimed at enabling students to think for themselves."

Often, students ask faculty, "What do I need to know to pass this course?" They don't wish to be burdened with extraneous information. It is as if education were merely memorizing a series of facts to be faithfully regurgitated at examination time and promptly forgotten. Courses in such a scenario resemble more a fraternity initiation than an education.

Education versus Indoctrination

Such education resembles a smorgasbord rather than an environment promoting independent thinking. A rationale for current thinking is that students must have the ability to shape their own program and not feel bound to a rigid series of courses. Often the result is that some take the path of least resistance, opting for courses offered at a convenient time that will provide the least stress.

That attitude is indicative of student immaturity. Rather than considering them as "consumers," the institution should view them as immature young adults needing guidance from faculty to become focused. Many are unclear what they hope to achieve through college education, except, of course, a good-paying job.

That situation can be especially true in liberal arts, and less so in the physical sciences, engineering, and the health professions where knowledge in certain specialties must be mastered. But even in those areas, reasoning has assumed diminished importance. Bertrand Russell's dictum, "The goal of education is to teach students how to think, not what to think," is no longer a priority even at prestigious schools.

What Does Diversity Include?

The term diversity has become a buzzword in the lexicon of academic administrators. By definition, the term refers to "the condition of being different or having differences." From an educational standpoint, its purpose is to expose students to others of different racial, religious, and ethnic backgrounds as well as a diversity of ideas and

Failed Grade

concepts that will prepare them to function effectively in a multicultural environment.

However, the current viewpoint is narrowly focused with the opinion that faculty members, staff, administrators, and students should mirror the ethnic, religious, and racial make-up of American society. Yet, there is no objective confirmation that the learning environment is improved by this narrow focus. To achieve this objective, some institutions have begun establishing centers of diversity, though no one has enunciated how these centers will enhance student education in various academic disciplines. It is as though population diversity itself is its own raison d'être. Diversity has an important role in educating the next generation. The main reason is to expose students to diverse concepts and ideas provided by those with different backgrounds and experiences. Thereby, they challenge their own preconceived biases while broadening their education by sensitizing them to another's background. It is a worthwhile objective.

Yet, many liberal arts departments in colleges and universities focus on recruiting faculty who are "compatible" philosophically and mirror images of existing faculty. In this regard, viewpoint diversity is not prized, only ethnic diversity. The result is entire departments become over-specialized, narrow-minded, and monolithic. A "politically correct" mentality infuses such departments whether from the left or right. These are, as David Bromwich calls them,[6] "The New Fundamentalists." The rare faculty member who was inadvertently recruited and does not fit the desired mold is made to feel uncomfortable.

Education versus Indoctrination

At the time for a tenure decision, spurious arguments can be offered to deny keeping that person in the unit.

Students in such an atmosphere become indoctrinated and not educated. They are not exposed to the diversity of ideas from the faculty. They are discouraged from thinking independently and challenging existing dogma or faculty and departmental views. Consequently, they receive an inferior education.

It is ironic that many senior faculty members in such departments were educated in the Vietnam era or immediately thereafter. They had experienced opprobrium for their ideas then by the existing establishment. Yet, they have now recreated their own orthodoxy and intolerance. Intellectual diversion by others in the group from their strongly held positions is discouraged, overtly or implicitly.

Education in a Changing Environment

Since knowledge is continually being created and new concepts are always replacing existing ones, a college education should provide a student with a background that will withstand this continually changing environment. In my own field, I've seen established drugs relegated to the ash heap and replaced by completely new ones that could not have been imagined. Yet, I've heard students say, "I know what I need to know to practice." That is a naïve and myopic viewpoint and must be continually challenged. The knowledge base must not be narrow if one is attempting to prepare a student for a professional lifespan of forty-five to fifty years.

Failed Grade

Learning to think independently is clearly of greater importance than memorizing a series of facts. I learned this in my first year in graduate school. In my last year as an undergraduate, I had taken an advanced course in organic chemistry. It was an area of chemistry in which I wanted to major. One of my professors in that discipline had a photographic memory, and when he forgot his notes, he still filled up the blackboards with series of equations. We students busily copied what he provided us. His examinations were merely a regurgitation of the facts he had given us. My final grade in his course was a 98.

I thought I knew organic chemistry when I entered graduate school. But when I enrolled and took the department's graduate entrance examination, I failed the organic chemistry part! The chemistry department required that I repeat and pass that portion of the examination within six months to remain in the program. That I did. In retrospect, my undergraduate background in that area was obviously poor. I had been taught to memorize a series of facts and not to think and reason as Bertrand Russell had suggested. That failure was a great learning experience, making me a more effective teacher. I realized that learning facts cannot be equated with knowledge and reasoning. Being able to apply one's knowledge to the solution of new problems is what education is all about.

Assessing Quality Programs

There are two important questions to ask in considering a college education. What should one expect a college education to provide? And how can one determine the

Education versus Indoctrination

location of quality programs? A college education needs to stress a student's intellectual abilities, the capacity to reason and comprehend, skills in thinking and problem-solving and strong ethical underpinnings. It should provide students with the background necessary to cope with the myriad problems that they will face in a professional lifetime. Clearly this can be a major disadvantage to online universities and distance learning as currently constituted.

The critical question is: how can one identify places where education and not indoctrination is provided? Parents and students would like answers to that question. As in similar questions, it is easier to determine inferior programs than to identify institutions where superior education can be found.

Educational establishments are now using the techniques of Madison Avenue to merchandise their programs,[7] encourage students to apply, and promote their programs and degrees so, caveat emptor. Program reputation is based on the past and not current information. Seeing an institution and its facilities is no guide as to the quality of the educational experience. Education comes from people—faculty, other students and administrators—and not from facilities. Even sitting in on a lecture or a class is not a true measure of an institution's academic environment.

Courses offered at institutions may have a political or social agenda and not an educational purpose. The problem that institutions have is how can they ensure that all courses are concerned with student education and prevent the small fraction of faculty focused on indoctrination? It is not

Failed Grade

simple, because the issue posed brings to the fore freedom of speech and faculty prerogatives in teaching. It is necessary that students appreciate the complexities and nuances in many pressing social and political issues and acquire the maturity to examine these objectively, using all of the information available.

In the final analysis, it is the faculty who must ensure such objectivity, decrying those who wish to inculcate their own biases. No educational institution should allow courses under its aegis whose purpose is indoctrination. This reflects poorly not only on the institution and its administration but on faculty members as well. Colleges and universities with little institutional control regarding what faculty members wish to offer present a prescription for disaster.

Institutions have a responsibility to expect that all courses are objective, have been thoroughly researched, approved by an independent faculty committee, and have a clear educational purpose. And all students should be encouraged to enroll. Otherwise, why should such courses be offered?

What are some of the other issues to be examined by students in evaluating an institution? When considering an undergraduate program, it is desirable to determine whether the lectures and recitation sections are offered by faculty members or graduate assistants. The latter, obviously, are not as knowledgeable on subject matter or accomplished in presentation as faculty members. In this regard, it is also useful to determine the percentage of a faculty member's time devoted to undergraduate education versus research,

Education versus Indoctrination

graduate education, and administration. In programs where generating grant support is important, certain faculty may devote little time to undergraduates. It isn't only the quality of the faculty that is important but their availability and commitment to undergraduate education.

Program quality is the key measure of a good institution. Probably the best gauge of a program's quality is its perception by recent graduates. They are in a position to determine how effective their education has been by comparison with others from different programs and institutions. The key problem is obtaining unbiased information. Obviously, that is not an easy task since institutions want to project themselves in the best possible light.

Finally, it is not unusual to make decisions with incomplete information. One learns of the institution's ambience only in retrospect. However, every institution has faculty who feel privileged to be able to educate the next generation. These individuals care about students. It is the students' responsibility to seek them out in order to maximize their own education. Recalling[8] what Andrew D. White, first president of Cornell University, said to an entering freshman class, "You are not here to receive an education. You are here to educate yourselves."

Chapter Nine
The Problem with the Leadership-Selection Process

The problems in leadership selection are everywhere. Geraldine Laybourne, Chairman and CEO of Oxygen Media Inc., said she learned more from her worse bosses than her better ones. She was taking notes on how not to manage. The worst leaders for me were also highly instructive.

Before examining them in colleges and universities, I want to examine why an individual wants to be an academic administrator, what the motivating factors are. Can anybody aspire to become an academic administrator, never having served in a faculty position?

Failed Grade

Background and Motivation for Academic Administrators

Certainly there are administrative positions in colleges that do not require previous experience as a faculty member. Having the requisite background, for example, in finance for a fiscal officer, is obviously of greater importance than having worked in a college. Although the function of such individuals is vital for institutional success, nevertheless, they are peripheral to the main mission of a college, namely the education of students.

Therefore, the focus in this book is on academic administrators. These individuals are concerned with the recruitment and retention of faculty; with evaluation of faculty and staff directly involved with academic programs; with program development and the establishment of academic standards; with the selection, motivation, advising, mentoring, and monitoring of students; and finally, with budgetary responsibility to meet the academic goals.

It is vital they have had experience as full-time faculty members. One might ask why that is essential. Isn't administration the same regardless of where practiced? Academic administration is especially demanding. This is due to the responsibility of leading, motivating, and monitoring bright and generally articulate faculty members whose relationship with the institution through tenure transcends and modifies the level of control academic administrators may have.

The faculty member's relationship with the institution after achieving tenure can affect the relationship with an

106

The Problem with the Leadership-Selection Process

administrator and the latter's leverage on the faculty member's attitudes and performances. But that is as it should be, since controlling faculty should not be the objective of any academic administrator, but creating an environment where faculty can function effectively is. In order to have credibility and support from faculty, it is essential that an administrator have firsthand knowledge of what being a highly productive faculty member means. This experience is indispensable in creating an effective environment for teaching and scholarship within any unit.

That idea is changing, according to Robert C. and Jon Solomon in their book, *Up the University: Re-creating Higher Education in America.* They state,[1] "A corollary of the management revolution was the idea *a good manager can manage anything.* It is not surprising then, that many university administrators are no longer professors or ex-deans but former city managers, state bureaucrats, up-and-coming politicians, and semi-retired or would-be corporate executives." In the current corporate environment that may be true, but from experience, I think that non-academics cannot be effective academic administrators without practical experience of teaching and scholarly activities in colleges and universities.

Motivation for Administrative Positions
The motivation to become an administrator is as varied as the number of individuals applying and ultimately selected. For some, there is a waning interest in teaching or scholarship; for others it seems a logical step after becoming a full professor; for still others there is the power

Failed Grade

and control that is attractive; and finally some are motivated by poor leadership they have experienced.

As in all endeavors, there are excellent administrators and poor ones. Contemplating such a career, how would one know whether one possessed the attributes to make a good academic administrator? What are these? Are they learned or basically innate? What can be done to improve administrative skills on the one hand, while recognizing glaring deficiencies in potential applicants on the other? Such questions have confronted many search committees.

Selection Process

Before probing those attributes, let's consider the selection process that has a bearing on the types of individuals ultimately chosen. The typical selection process is for the senior administrator to choose a committee that will assist in identifying, screening, and interviewing potential candidates. The selection of that committee is no trivial matter. Obviously, the senior administrator wants individuals who are conscientious, have high academic standards, and, by their presence on the committee, are capable of attracting to campus highly qualified individuals. The committee initially begins as a composite of individuals with different backgrounds from various constituencies that must be molded into a single entity with a common mission.

The group's chemistry will determine its success or failure. For this committee does not play merely an advisory role, it has responsibility for providing the senior administrator with a list of candidates it deems satisfactory.

The Problem with the Leadership-Selection Process

If none of the individuals listed meet the expectations of the administrator, a new committee might be formed, or the existing committee asked to continue the search process.

The selection committee should be an independent entity and is not required to share with the senior administrator its inner deliberations. Only when its responsibilities are completed and a listing of candidates' names is submitted to the senior administrator is the committee's role finished. Generally, the administrator wants more than one name on the list to be able to exercise judgment in the selection process. However, as the corporate structure has taken hold, senior administrators are becoming conspicuously involved in these search committees.

An example will illustrate the point. A president was seeking an important senior dean for one of the health science programs. Once an applicant was found whom the president liked, he took over. The committee became irrelevant and no longer served its function. He negotiated directly with the candidate. When an overzealous president subverts the search process, no one will want to waste their time serving on committees.

The selection of academic administrators is highly convoluted. The process has been skewed by past injustices. Many decades ago, only white Christian males, preferably Protestants of Anglo-Saxon heritage, were considered for academic administrative positions. Non-Christians, women, Blacks and Hispanics weren't even on the radar screen. Now there is a more inclusive process. Equal opportunity and affirmative action principles are incorporated, and the process has become more formalized.

Failed Grade

Multiple inputs from many segments of the academic community are actively solicited. And though the process can be long and cumbersome, once completed, there is little complaint since the views of many have been sought.

However, many of these search committees have become too large in order to accommodate every constituency, and an unintended consequence is committees are too ponderous to be workable. Establishment of regular meeting times is not possible, nor can the chemistry be created among members leading to an effective committee. Collegiality is important in distributing tasks to committee members and ensuring its work will be completed in a timely manner. Committees larger than five to seven individuals are simply counterproductive. But, limiting the committee size places greater responsibility on all committee members in guaranteeing the search process is fair, inclusive, and does not perpetuate biases of the past.

Because of committee immobilization through size, following the corporate model, administrators and boards have turned to search firms for positions, such as president, provost, and various vice presidents. Unfortunately, this development has its downside since search firms select someone having broad appeal to a diverse committee.[2] Academic giants of a bygone era with a vision of the future are nowhere to be found. They probably wouldn't survive the first cut. For president committees now want a public relations master, a glad-hander, an excellent communicator, and above all a supreme fundraiser. One sees individuals, who were ineffective deans and provosts, offered positions

110

The Problem with the Leadership-Selection Process

as vice president for academic affairs and president. I doubt whether phone calls are ever made to faculty and administrators who were not the candidate's close friends, at institutions where the applicant had been.

I knew an eminent researcher on a search committee for dean of his college. He asked my frank opinion regarding a person whom I had known professionally for many years. I did not have a very flattering view of the candidate and his commitment in support of research. My views were clearly disquieting to this colleague, who thanked me for my frankness. Needless to say, I would not have shared those views with someone I did not know from a search firm. Also, the current litigious environment would have precluded such candor.

In another search, faculty at another institution complained to a colleague for failing to alert them about the undesirable qualities of a newly named president. The president had been at the institution where this colleague was. He retorted no one on the search committee had asked his opinion. The recycling of failed administrators has been a damaging consequence of expanded search committees and the need for outside search firms.

One problem in the search process is the failure of upper administration to communicate fully with the committee. After identifying the position to be filled, it is necessary for the committee to know: (1) managerial hierarchy, (a) to whom that person will be reporting and (b) who will be reporting to that person; (2) authority for hiring and firing; and (3) budgetary responsibility. If the organization doesn't know the responsibilities for the new administrator, it is

111

Failed Grade

impossible to communicate any objectives to possible applicants.

An example will illustrate this point. A president decided to create the new position of vice president for health sciences. Unfortunately, there was no carefully crafted job description that outlined the personnel and budgetary responsibilities, who would be reporting to this individual, and most importantly, how this position would interact with existing positions, such as other senior vice presidents. As a consequence, though excellent applicants came to campus, not one was interested in the position.

Interviews on campus of external candidates must be carefully planned for two main reasons. First, it is imperative to learn as much as one can of the administrative attributes of the candidate. Does the candidate have the wisdom, sensitivity, drive, temperament, and vision to be a successful academic leader?[3] This is the time when committee members individually and collectively decide if the person is a viable candidate. Time must be carefully structured to maximize the candidate's exposure and increase input from many segments of the academic community.

Secondly, the committee's role is to impress a candidate with the quality of the institution. One cannot assume that the candidate, if offered the position, will come. Moving to a new location can be stimulating but at the same time traumatic. It means leaving friends and sometimes even family members. It can be difficult for a spouse and children. The responsibility of the committee is to present

The Problem with the Leadership-Selection Process

the institution in the most favorable light, preserving for itself the option of accepting or rejecting any candidate.

The interview time is also a crucial time for the candidate. It is amazing how an innocent remark can undermine an individual's candidacy without the person being aware of what had happened. It may not be the remark itself, but how members of the committee viewed that comment. I remember an instance involving a candidate for a dean's position. The candidate was a very bright, articulate person, with a strong level of accomplishment in research and a clear understanding of her discipline. The interview process was going very well, and most committee members were clearly impressed with her. If the committee had voted early in the interview process, she would have been recommended.

A committee member then asked her in an offhand manner what were her career plans for the future. She was forthright in stating that she had enjoyed research, but was interested now in the challenges posed by administration. And since she was fifty-two, this would probably be her last professional position. It was an innocent remark and undoubtedly factual. For some members, however, this was an implicit statement she was seeking a position from which she would retire. Suddenly, the atmosphere within the committee changed from support to opposition.

This illustrates how challenging the interview time can be and how perceptions can influence a candidate's viability. Obviously, one should only make statements reflecting one's true feelings and values. But these must strike a responsive chord among committee members if the

113

Failed Grade

candidate is to retain the option of the position. It is difficult for anyone to know how comments to the committee members will be perceived.

One sensitive problem encountered in any administrative search is the application of internal candidates for an administrative position. These are colleagues who will likely remain at the institution whether or not selected for the position. It is important to be sensitive, even if the individuals are not viewed as serious candidates, since their cooperation with the new administrator will be important.

Timing for Administrative Positions

A final point worth mentioning relates to timing. I sense many people become administrators too early in their professional careers. For most people a ten-year time period as an administrator at a particular position is probably optimal.

Such a span is generally sufficient to formulate and undertake new initiatives, to provide fresh dynamism for faculty and staff, and to create a solid base for further development by succeeding administrators. The demands upon the academic administrator are great, and "burn-out" is frequent. Staying beyond an optimal time can be counterproductive not only for the individual, but also for the unit itself.

Change in administrative leadership can be both stimulating and unsettling. For certain faculty and staff, who have become complacent with an existing administrator, such a change can have a positive effect. People are insecure with new leadership and strive to show

The Problem with the Leadership-Selection Process

their abilities to the fullest. A certain amount of insecurity is desirable for all, since too much security can breed complacency and laziness. Renewal is a beneficial process for any organization and especially for academic institutions.

The aspiring administrator might ask during the succeeding eight-to-ten-year time span, "What will I do for an encore?" Unfortunately, some have few options. As a result, many administrators stay long after they have outlived their usefulness to the organization. I knew of a dean who served for more than twenty-five years. His drive of the past was gone, together with new ideas. Yet, he had no other options and remained in his administrative position longer than he should have.

Appointing individuals too early to senior administrative positions cannot help but produce administrative gridlock to the detriment of the individual and the organization. Dynamism and vision, of course, are not solely age dependent; those are more a function of personality. But appointing people to administrative positions later in their professional lives serves two important purposes.

First, there is a guarantee there will be timely administrative turnover. And second, the individual has a longer track record by which one can judge the person's accomplishments and potentiality for administrative success. Youth is no substitute for maturity, since experiences, some of which are frank failures, mold the future administrator. I learned more from my failures than my successes as an academic administrator. At the time I

Failed Grade

left administration, I had greater administrative ability than when I began.

It is rarely stated what is expected from the academic administrator, especially at the upper echelons. How will the person be judged before being reappointed? Just as students are asked to evaluate faculty, so too should senior administrators be evaluated by those who are reporting to them. Included in evaluation should not only be department chairs and deans, but also provosts and presidents.

Faculty should evaluate senior administrators as well as others functioning in the environment the administrators have created. Rarely does the board of trustees initiate an objective review of administrators, especially at the level of president and provost. And if done at all, the outcome can be predetermined, especially if those asking for the evaluation are "comfortable" with the person. Yet, it is at those levels where critical input from various constituencies is sorely needed.

As a result, the institution itself is at risk especially in today's corporate environment. Since all decisions of importance emanate from the top of the institution, who will evaluate the wisdom of those decisions? The lack of effective oversight of leadership has important consequences for the future of an institution.

Chapter Ten
Attributes for Administrative Success and Failure

In this chapter, I want to examine attributes and styles contributing to success and failure of academic administrators. The comment of Professor Henry Mintzberg[1] of McGill University School of Management, "Leadership, like swimming, cannot be learned by reading about it," is true. Yet, by focusing on attributes of successful and unsuccessful administrators, the selection process can be improved.

Desirable administrative attributes are not solely determined by the corporate or collegial structure. Much more a factor is an individual's personality and sensitivity to people with whom he or she is interacting, both those above and below in the organization's hierarchy. Oftentimes it is easier, though not better, to function in the corporate environment, where all decisions flow from the

Failed Grade

top. However, it is pertinent by contrast to show the strengths and weaknesses of the collegial environment in decision making.

By and large successful administrators are outgoing, gregarious people with a knack for relating to students, faculty, staff, alumni, and other administrators, even those with different personalities from their own. The successful ones create an open environment with a good esprit de corps, i.e., a collegial environment. They foster an individual's optimism and commitment to the organization, which leads to their enhanced productivity and the organization's success. On the other hand, those who are highly introverted are usually not successful administratively, regardless of brilliance. The continuing challenge for administrators is to develop and maintain a productive and dynamic environment—no easy task in any organization. Though Rhodes in his book, *The Creation of the Future*, discusses the attributes of the university president,[2] his comments apply to any senior academic administrator.

Normally, one socializes with people with whom one works. Such relationships for academic administrators can become complicated. Since other people in the administrative unit are dependent upon the administrator for their positions, promotions, space, and salary increases, it can be difficult to separate one's role as a supervisor from that of a friend. Even if that were possible, there is the issue of perceptions. The administrator is in the proverbial goldfish bowl, always under scrutiny by others in the unit. Perceptions can become reality. The perception of

Attributes for Administrative Success and Failure

favoritism, even when untrue, is detrimental to the organization. Not only must the administrator be fair and impartial, but there must be that perception as well. Therefore, the administrative role can be very isolating not only socially but also professionally. It can be difficult knowing whether associates are being truthful regarding the administrator's ideas or are currying favors.

It is important for an effective administrator to have a high degree of sensitivity and respect for someone else's ideas. Even though one has vision and strives to enhance the university's contribution to students, research/scholarship and society, without sensitivity and respect of others, one may fail to recognize the insecurities besetting those in the organization. One can be the proverbial "bull in a china shop," incapable of maximizing the contributions of others, and thereby lose some of the better people. In essence, one's antennae must be very sensitive to weak signals. A corollary of this statement, one must be a good listener to be an effective administrator.

It is important to understand the views of others, whether or not one agrees with them. Listening to people can uncover personal agendas that may not be the true reasons for those opinions. For example, in the recruitment of faculty, those who are not engaged in scholarly activities can feel threatened by recruiting someone with an excellent research program. To hide one's insecurities, the candidate's commitment to teaching could be challenged as the basis for opposing selection. Obfuscating one's real objectives is a common approach, and an effective

119

Failed Grade

administrator must be capable of seeing through such tactics by bright and articulate colleagues.

The most critical requirement for any administrator is adherence to strong ethical principles. The administrator's dealings with subordinates, faculty, staff, students, and alumni, as well as those in superior administrative positions, must be based on honesty and trust. In Chapter 13, "Ethics and the Administrator," more time is devoted to this issue. The promises of devious and unprincipled administrators cannot be relied on, creating a bad academic climate.

If decision making is important, then creating an atmosphere where constructive criticism and new ideas can flourish is crucial. Welcoming criticism is an important attribute. To foster such an environment, the administrator must demonstrate that criticism by others, and contrary viewpoints are welcome even if the ultimate decision runs counter to those positions. Actions speak louder than words. An important litmus test is how an administrator deals with criticism.

If administrators treat subordinates differently, based on their agreement or disagreement with the administrator's positions, people will support whatever the administrator says or remain silent. Administrators frequently surround themselves with individuals they refer to as "team players." This term is a euphemism for sycophants who seek to ingratiate themselves. The real "team player" is one who expresses views honestly but once a decision has been made works to implement it, regardless of whether it is contrary to his or her own.

Attributes for Administrative Success and Failure

The single most important function of any administrator is the recruitment of associates, since they will play a major role in the success or failure of that administration. For this purpose, the administrator must have good judgment and be willing to spend the time to find, recruit, support, and retain quality individuals. The best indicator of competence is the type of associates selected and success in retaining the best people. The Uriah Heeps of this world contribute little to any administration.

In the chapter titled "How Flatterers Are to be Fled" in his book *The Prince*, Niccolo Machiavelli has observed,[3] "Choosing wise men in his state, and only to those must he (the prince) give license to speak the truth to him, and of those things alone that he asks about and of nothing else; but he must ask them about everything, and hear their opinions; thereafter to deliberate alone, in his own way." Wise and honest associates better serve every administrator. Their selection is indicative of the administrator's security and confidence. I've seen new administrators rid themselves of holdovers, even some excellent people. These bosses view loyalty to them as more important than competency. That does not augur well for the future.

An important administrative attribute is being able to create an effective environment for others. The administrator creates the atmosphere for the organization, and this is accomplished by example, not by directive. There are basically two types of administrators: (1) those who wish to serve and (2) those who wish to be served. The former are to be prized. The latter frequently have two

Failed Grade

standards, one for themselves and one for everyone else. Creating such an environment does not engender commitment by others to the institution. The focus becomes solely on "number one" and there is little value in cooperating with others. Establishing a good esprit de corps minimizes the loss of good faculty and staff, as well as achieving excellent learning conditions for students. The self-serving administrator does neither.

Another attribute that generates confidence and trust is transparency or openness in decision making. If the process is a transparent one, even if the final decision is not fully supported by everyone, openness[4] creates a more trusting environment than one in which very little is shared. We can't help the type of people we are, but an administrator unable or unwilling to share thought processes creates unease.

The growth of one's associates should be another objective. They must learn to solve problems and recognize pitfalls in decision making. Insecure administrators arrogate to themselves all decisions and their implementation. But time is the major limitation and by being involved in every single decision, even if competent associates could handle them, an administrator is utilizing time poorly as well as that of associates. Conversely, the administrator who delegates all problems is unfair and unwise. The role of the effective administrator is to use judgment in determining which problems can be delegated and which should be handled personally.

In this context, it is important that once a problem has been delegated, the decision making responsibility now

Attributes for Administrative Success and Failure

rests with the associate. The associate must keep the administrator apprised of the process, possible disposition of the problem, and how it can be dealt with in a timely fashion. Those time parameters should be reasonable and indicated at the outset.

Some administrators give the same problem to several people, creating unnecessary confusion. Once an associate has made and implemented a decision, it must be fully supported by the administrator, especially in public, even if the senior person would have handled the matter differently. It is important to share those reasons with the associate in private. The only way an associate can learn is by doing, and making mistakes is a normal part of the learning process. It is important to instill responsibility in an associate. Knowing the administrator has delegated both responsibility, as well as authority, engenders caution in addition to confidence.

The development of an administrator is much like educating a graduate student to become a researcher. It takes time, experience, and the making of mistakes. One should acknowledge in public the accomplishments of an associate; it is wrong to take personal credit for every decision. What one can take credit for is selecting and helping develop associates.

Patience is a key virtue for the administrator. The two sides of the coin are patience and impatience. The solving of a complicated problem can be very time consuming. The goal is not to get the problem off one's desk, but to solve it fairly and equitably so as to improve the organization's

Failed Grade

effectiveness. More important than making a decision is making the correct decision that has longevity.

Part of the process should involve deliberation, even vacillation. The process must run its course irrespective of the administrator's impatience. Some administrators are under the illusion that it is more important to demonstrate decisiveness than deliberation. They want to show "who's in charge" rather than solving the problem effectively. Many would-be administrators are impatient and time-oriented rather than goal-oriented. As H. L. Mencken said, "For every complex, difficult problem, there is a simple, easy solution—and it's wrong."

Impatience can be both a vice and a virtue. One can be too deliberate, resulting in a dilatory administration, incapable of making and implementing any decision. By postponing a decision, one is making a decision. Harvey Cox, the theologian, has said, "...not to decide is to decide." Achieving a balance between patience and impatience is very important for the successful administrator.

The administrator must not be dictatorial in academic decisions where faculty must make judgments. However, the administrator has a perfect right to set reasonable time parameters when the decision must be made. A criticism of the collegial structure versus the corporate model is that the former is too slow. If faculty members don't reach a decision in a timely manner, the fault is with the administrator who failed to establish reasonable deadlines at the outset.

Attributes for Administrative Success and Failure

Related is the fact that the administrative role should be viewed as a facilitative one. Every individual in administration has a responsibility to aid others—students, faculty, and staff—to achieve their objectives. This can be accomplished when the environment is supportive of everyone. Problems, which impede the creation of a collegial atmosphere, must be dealt with administratively. In the corporate structure, this is less important. By emphasizing service to others, one connotes administrative importance of cooperation and collegiality. If the objective is developing a productive organization, service by administration must be perceived as a high priority.

Another attribute of the effective administrator is intolerance of persistent incompetence. Everyone makes mistakes; however, if faculty or staff members are continually ineffective, their incompetence should not be tolerated. It is amazing how many incompetents are retained. There are a variety of reasons, but among these is administrative laziness. There is also the realization that terminating a person's position will be unpleasant, time-consuming, and may have political and legal ramifications.

Accepting incompetence is a defect of both collegial and corporate structures, especially when mistakes were made at the time of tenure or permanence for staff positions. But tolerance of incompetence is itself incompetence. Others must compensate for this failure. An administrator with low tolerance for incompetence better serves the institution. Administrators immobilized by potential litigation don't belong in administration. A greater concern should be doing the ethical and correct thing for the organization and

Failed Grade

if, in the process, one is sued in a worthy cause then so be it.

Lastly, an important administrative attribute is a sense of humor. The "all business," humorless individual creates a dreary and tiring environment. There are times when levity, even at one's own expense, permits others to exit from difficult situations. Humor is a powerful lubricant, and its absence can create friction and exacerbate tensions.

Related is an ability not to take oneself too seriously. It is important for the administrators to remember that there were other administrators on the scene before they arrived and there will be others after they are gone. No one is indispensable. I jested with my wife that if I had suddenly expired, administrators above me would express great sadness, but would wonder, in the same breath, who should become the next interim college administrator? This statement is not meant to be critical or reflect insensitivity but to illustrate the need for administrative continuity. It is useful to realize that one's own time as an administrator is finite, that responsibility is not granted in perpetuity. Too many administrators become overly impressed with themselves.[5] They fail to realize that the only water that anyone of us can walk on is ice and that is always treacherous.

Chapter Eleven
First Days on the Job

"In the saddle" seems an appropriate term as one assumes administrative responsibility. Though this discussion may seem a departure from a description of environment and attributes of leadership, I intend it to provide further insight into responsibilities and actions of administrators. A person might wonder what should be done first in a new administrative position. Before long a myriad of questions, requests, and requirements for action begin to demand time.

Ideally, one should prioritize time and to set one's own agenda. Perhaps in the corporate setting that is possible, but not in a collegial environment where service to others and the organization is overriding. Setting one's time agenda doesn't occur. One cannot be shut away. That perception can be detrimental to achieving the unit's objectives.

On the other hand, there is a need for uninterrupted time, examining problem areas. There must be a balance between

Failed Grade

instant and very restricted accessibility by others. Achieving that balance is not always easy. The single most important thing is establishing a relationship with each individual directly reporting to the administrative office. Collectively, they will contribute to the administrator's success. When moving to a new place, I found it was effective to meet personally with each individual reporting directly to me.

I did this over two months. I asked three questions: (1) what did they perceive as the single most important issue adversely affecting the unit; (2) what were their own professional aspirations; and (3) how could I help them achieve those goals? Perhaps there are other questions but these appeared the most pertinent to me when assuming a new position without having historical background.

The first question was important in problem identification. It provided me with an academic mosaic permitting me to gain insight as to the unit's problems and strengths. Though I had my own perspective, I wanted to validate it. The coupling of these two perspectives provided a solid foundation on which to prioritize those issues that must be dealt with early on. Also, it demonstrated their opinions were valued. In these discussions, I gained a firsthand exposure as to the substantial people in the unit.

With faculty members, I focused on their teaching and scholarly accomplishments. Knowing who were creative among the faculty and staff was important. I knew these individuals would be needed in solving problems and planning for the future.

First Days on the Job

In this regard, it is important to discuss with one's predecessor the critical issues affecting the unit. After all, he or she had been grappling with these for a long period of time. Obtaining that opinion did not mean these matters would have the same importance to me or that I had to proceed in the same manner as my predecessor. However, information is important in formulating an agenda for dealing with issues that must be addressed. As indicated, multiple inputs are essential in these early days. Frequently, new administrators want to dissociate themselves completely from the past. But not using all resources available seems a lack of judgment or indicative of insecurity. However, meeting and listening to one's predecessor does not mean the new administration is to be a continuation of the past.

Problem identification is important. Then comes the question of what to do in solving these problems. It is a normal assumption for new administrators to feel each problem has a solution. A related question is, are they worth solving? Resolution of some problems may require the full support and involvement of one's superiors.

The other two questions relate to the individual's own goals. Gaining an insight as to what faculty are currently doing in teaching and scholarship and what the different activities of the staff are helps in determining the unit's strengths and weaknesses. The interview meeting demonstrates the administrator cares about each person's development and that their role is not merely to serve the administrator's needs. Relationships are a "two-way"

Failed Grade

street—one cannot expect loyalty if the administrator is not prepared to give it first.

In all organizations, there are a variety of people. Some faculty will be consumed with their research careers and view teaching and service responsibilities as a necessary evil. This attitude is common in the recruitment of self-absorbed entrepreneurial faculty. Others may confine themselves to teaching, and their interest in scholarship has waned. Still others are committed to both. Some may be gravitating toward administrative careers. And a few have effectively retired while still drawing a paycheck. How to motivate the latter has been a serious but not impossible challenge in academia.

In addition to faculty, meeting with senior staff is essential. With each person, one gets an insight as to their objectives and how the administrator might enhance the person's contribution to the unit's development. These meetings are a beginning in a relationship. Difficulties stemming from human relations must be examined to improve satisfaction and productivity.[1]

It is important also to reach out to students and alumni. Putting students at ease to probe strengths and weaknesses of programs should be undertaken. Students don't want to be negative, especially with a new administrator, fearing repercussions from faculty. However, interviewing the brightest students can provide valuable insight, identifying the better teachers and program deficiencies.

Similarly, alumni are an important resource, not merely for fundraising but in understanding the status of a particular career or profession. These may be practitioners

First Days on the Job

and help the administrator determine programmatic changes that should be considered. Meetings connote too that their opinions are valued.

Listening of course doesn't imply their suggestions will be endorsed or implemented. It is a source of information. I remember one alumnus complained regarding the typing abilities of our pharmacy graduates, and he suggested instituting a typing course. I listened respectfully with no intention to accede since I did not view typing as a course for college credit. With the computer, such concerns are irrelevant now.

Informal discussions with various groups also provide a forum for hearing new ideas. Some administrators have decided on their own agenda and can't learn from anyone else. But such people have serious limitations that will adversely affect the unit's future.

Another matter of importance for the administrator is the unit's budget and how to maximize its use. Budgets in colleges largely involve personnel with percentages as high as ninety. Thus, an administrator may have little flexibility in shaping the budget unless there is a reduction in personnel. Paring administrative costs and the resulting bureaucracy should be undertaken early in one's administration since recovered resources can be used for teaching and scholarly activities. It is desirable to view one's role in the budget as the unit's custodian with prudent use for the benefit of all. That is the administrator's fiscal responsibility. Administrative travel, accommodations, and their expenses should be justified by the same criteria as applied to others in the unit.

131

Failed Grade

Unfortunately that's not always the case. One president I knew took the basketball team and many of his staff to a foreign country. He was in the position to do so since there was meaningless oversight from the board of trustees. The money reputedly came from non-university sources. But since all money is green, resources could have been better spent on the institution's needs. Or if use were restricted to athletic programs, the number of scholarships for needy students could have been increased.

The expenditure of monies must not only be fair and equitable but give that perception as well. Many administrators use the unit's budget as if it were their own bank account. They travel extensively to meetings and places that are unnecessary to the institution's mission. That money would be better spent by sending faculty to professional or scientific meetings that may improve their teaching and scholarship. At the same time, the administrator would have more time in the office addressing issues that must be dealt with and gain a greater appreciation of the environment under which others are working.

Some administrators greatly limit or ration access by faculty, staff, and students. Essentially, they have created a closed-door policy, isolating themselves from others. By such actions they are indicating they are too busy to meet with these groups and the perception is that their needs and opinions are not critical to the unit's success.

Some administrators don't want to be surprised by any issue and want to know beforehand the reasons an individual wants to meet with them. That requirement is

First Days on the Job

commonplace in the corporate environment. It is perfectly permissible for any administrator to indicate the need for time to consider any request before responding. That response should be done in a timely manner.

Though e-mail is a boon to communicating, it is also a way of isolating an administrator from faculty and staff. In effect, communication becomes highly impersonal. By using it largely in place of one-on-one meetings, one doesn't see expressions or body language of people.

Obviously, e-mail and voice mail are useful when communicating with people in other buildings and institutions. However, using it as a substitute for face-to-face meetings with subordinates and associates, especially on sensitive and critical matters, is unwise. All administrators want to be shielded from unpleasant sessions, but that demonstrates a lack of courage and leadership, especially when such matters must be dealt with.

As a guide to communicating with those reporting to you, what kind of access would you want to your own bosses? Would you be happy communicating solely by e-mail or required to meet with an assistant having no authority for making decisions? I assume the response would be a negative one; then, one shouldn't establish a similar environment for subordinates.

At the outset, the administrator should set the tone of how he or she will communicate with people in the unit. An open environment fosters confidence and mitigates the influence of those individuals in every organization who

Failed Grade

are negative. Many people are generally distrustful of administrators, and restricted access feeds into that distrust.

Finally, after beginning to understand the unit and its strengths and weaknesses and after developing plans, it is important to share these views with one's administrative superiors. They should be asked for their comments. A brief written report to the superior is in order followed by a face-to-face meeting. Some matters may be too sensitive to put in writing and can be best discussed verbally.

Satisfactory communication with one's superiors and subordinates is the hallmark of a successful administrator. George Bernard Shaw quipped, "The greatest danger in communication is the illusion that it has been accomplished." This truism is especially important for anyone in administration. People cannot know one's intentions unless they are shared.

Unfortunately, it's my experience that there is extensive turnover in personnel at upper administration levels in colleges and universities. Continuity and institutional loyalty seem a thing of the past. Just as entrepreneurial faculty are now recruited, so too are entrepreneurial administrators. No sooner are they in one administrative position than they're positioning themselves for the next chapter in their career.

Chapter Twelve
Administrative Sensitivity

Faculty jest that the phrase "administrative sensitivity" is an oxymoron. This is most apparent in a corporate environment and the reduction of faculty in university governance and decision making. But effective administrators, even with marginal credentials, compensate for meager academic accomplishments through administrative sensitivity. One university president I knew had a knack for remembering the names of everyone he met months later. He worked a room of people as successfully as any politician. His skills were in public relations, and they were superb. Such skills are especially important in a corporate environment.

On one occasion, I was wrestling with the reappointment of a particular chair. The individual was dynamic, with good ideas, but he lacked the sensitivity to work with others outside his division in carrying out needed changes. I

Failed Grade

appreciated his limitations and tried on numerous occasions to make him aware of how his actions were perceived by others. When I talked to him in that light, he was incredulous. He said he never looked at the matter in that way. It was like trying to show a particular color to a color-blind person. C. E. Stowe has observed, "Common sense is the knack of seeing things as they are, and doing things as they ought to be done." Sensitivity to others was not my colleague's forte, and I was singularly unsuccessful in helping him become effective.

When the members in his division unanimously supported his reappointment for a new four-year term, I was inclined to accede to their recommendation though I had great reservations. In discussing this matter with an excellent colleague, he suggested I appoint him for one rather than four years. That way I was showing respect for the faculty, while putting the chair on notice that if he remained ineffective administratively, this would be his final year as chairman. It was an excellent idea, and I followed it. The chair was unhappy with my decision. But within a month, a sizeable delegation from his division complained about his weak interpersonal skills, asking that his administrative responsibilities be terminated. Fortunately, by limiting the duration of his appointment, damage in his role as chair was limited.

Related to sensitivity is openness and trust in decision making. I recall an instance in which it seemed desirable to coalesce two small units with related interests into a larger and hopefully more dynamic entity. The advantages

Administrative Sensitivity

seemed to outweigh the disadvantages. Among the gains were:

(1) a larger critical mass of faculty members;
(2) fewer committee assignments for each faculty member, since there was need for representation from each unit on committees;
(3) potential for more effective graduate student recruitment;
(4) securing and sharing joint equipment; and,
(5) development of curricula that would meet a changing environment.

The key question was not whether the change should be made but how to make it so there would be a degree of permanence. In my view, the faculty directly affected by this change should express their views. I indicated at the outset that if there were significant opposition to the merger, I would not initiate it again during the remainder of my administration.

In effect, I offered a window of opportunity for the merger, but pledged it would occur only with full faculty support. Initially, I met with each group separately, listened attentively to arguments both pro and con and the hidden and not-so-hidden agendas. Concerns expressed were: Who would chair the new unit? I said if a merger occurred, the combined faculty would make that decision. Would there be a reduction in secretarial support if the units merged? My answer was no. And finally, would the loss of a vote on the executive committee be critical? I indicated there would be no effect since the combined unit's views were important to the college. Insecurities had been placed

Failed Grade

directly on the table and dealt with as honestly and forthrightly as I could.

Subsequently, I asked each faculty member to vote by secret ballot for or against the merger. The vote overwhelmingly approved the union and it was implemented. Without administrative sensitivity and faculty support, any decision could have been counter-productive. It might have resulted in an environment where seeds for dissolution of the merged entity would have been planted.

The process of collegiality is time consuming. But speed is not the critical issue; the stability and longevity of administrative changes are. Unfortunately, in the corporate climate, there is diminishing administrative interest in faculty concerns and governance. Upper administrators view their role as one of unequivocal support of administrators reporting to them, regardless of performance. They are not being objective, failing to focus on the best interests of the unit and the institution.

From such situations, I've learned the importance of listening and the need for transparency in decision making. Credible administrators are successful ones. Also, I learned the importance of process in problem solving. Arriving at a decision is but the first step. Developing a process for the acceptance and implementation of decisions is as important as the decision itself. And a flawed process can undermine even a correct decision.

Chapter Thirteen
Ethics and the Administrator

The ethical treatment of people is important for every organization. As Chester I. Barnard said [1] in *The Functions of the Executive*, "Every executive possesses, independently of the position he occupies, personal moral codes." That also applies to academic administrators. Ethics in higher education has become an issue of increasing importance.[2]

At the outset, I'm certain all administrators want to create an ethical environment for everyone in their academic units. However, where decisions and actions are solely based on what one wishes to accomplish and ethical treatment of individuals becomes of secondary consideration, an unethical environment is created. The corporate culture with its overriding focus on the financial imperative can result in a negative impact on how individuals in the group are treated. As Amy Gutmann reminds us,[3] "Professionals, including professors and

Failed Grade

university administrators, have so many important and pressing purposes that it is practically difficult to stop and think about ethical principles before acting." Clearly then, ethical behavior must be innate or instilled as a high priority into aspiring administrators.

As stated, there are two types of administrators, those who serve and those who wish to be served. The latter give administrators a bad name. They manipulate the system for their own benefit. One president on leaving one institution for another, wanted to know all his perquisites at the first institution so these would be a condition for accepting the second presidency. Such administrators, who are self-serving, gauge everything by its benefit to themselves.

In my administrative role with faculty and staff, I sought always to follow the ancient advice of Rabbi Hillel (100 BCE), "Don't treat someone else the way that you would not wish to be treated." It made my administrative life easier since an absence of guile is what I wanted. People were entitled to know my thinking and that promises made would be carried out. I wanted an administrative environment without ambiguity. I used the same approach with those to whom I was reporting.

I endeavored to ensure that individuals accepting a position knew how they would be treated. I told them what they could expect. Verbal commitments were just that, commitments. I adhered to promises, but if a delay was required, I informed the individual in advance. People didn't need written commitments from me to ensure they would be honored. Even were ethical considerations not paramount, I spent a great deal of time recruiting and didn't

Ethics and the Administrator

want that time wasted. The departure of good faculty because of ethical lapses is indicative of weak administration. If one is unable to keep a promise, why make it? And where there are broken promises, such an administrator cannot be trusted with other commitments.

I cite two examples. In one, we recruited a well-qualified assistant professor, and in her acceptance she indicated her husband was completing his Ph.D. and would need a two-year post-doctoral appointment for her to come. After discussion with the chair of her division, it was agreed a temporary position should be provided. She was informed the position for her husband would be available when his Ph.D. was completed. This time provided him an opportunity to secure a more permanent position. We kept the commitment, and at the end of two years he obtained another position in a different unit within the university.

In the second instance, a newly recruited assistant professor accepted a verbal commitment without qualifications and received an offer. Weeks later he responded that he would only come if a laboratory position were available for his girlfriend. He hadn't been straightforward at the outset, placing additional conditions on his previous acceptance. I responded informing him the offer was withdrawn. In some two-career families now, administrative involvement is necessary to secure a position for a spouse or friend. Here that is not the issue. The matter is one of openness. The individual could have come and we would have helped him secure a position for his friend. But making that a new condition after already accepting the position was unacceptable.

Failed Grade

The concept of a permanent position seems now a relic of a bygone era. Mobility fed by entrepreneurship is occurring at every level in the university. Over a period of ten years as dean, I had six immediate bosses. Most who came as provost considered the position simply a way station to a presidency, and some began searching immediately after arriving on campus. There was no commitment to the institution. Such ethical problems have become commonplace. When senior administrators behave thus, others cannot be faulted for thinking in the same way. The person at the top sets the ethical tone for the institution. Loyalty and commitment are parts of a two-way street. To expect it from subordinates, administrators must demonstrate it first.

An analogy is the relationship of parents to children. Parents must provide unconditional love and commitment, creating an ethical environment for their children, regardless of how obedient or successful they are. Only in that atmosphere do loyalty and responsibility develop.

Unethical behavior is not confined to administrators. Some faculty members, having received institutional research support, depart for more prestigious universities, taking with them supplies and equipment provided by the former college. This attitude is exacerbated when institutions recruit "star" faculty who arrive with no interest in teaching and little commitment to the institution. Receiving a better offer elsewhere, they promptly leave. Though chastened by such "bad apples," the good administrator's ethical behavior must remain unaffected.

Ethics and the Administrator

People need to know, of course, how an administrator perceives them; yet it is wrong for administrators to assume a lack of criticism is indicative of their satisfaction. Some administrators are concerned that by being complimentary they are exposing themselves to unreasonable salary demands. But that is not necessarily true, since most faculty/staff recognize all institutions have financial constraints.

In one instance, I informed a tenured faculty member of unpleasant news. His area of expertise was less important than other specialties in the college. I informed him future salary increments would not be significant. I indicated I would not make his life intolerable but had to use the college's fiscal resources for the development of other areas that I thought more relevant. Rather than saying nothing, I treated him the way I would want to be treated. This individual remained in the college, undertaking national projects, giving him greater visibility. Ultimately, he was promoted to full professor.

One of my associate deans was an effective faculty member before assuming administrative responsibilities. Since he did an excellent job administratively, I continued to reward him with significant salary increases. When he retired he thanked me profusely since the increases had affected his retirement benefits. Many administrators, he said, would not have done that since people approaching retirement frequently receive only token raises.

An ethical administrator should always abide by the process that he or she has initiated. An example will illustrate this point. There was a research administrator

Failed Grade

with responsibility for a particular center. When time came to review the salary and reappointment of the center's administrator, the research administrator established a committee to evaluate his effectiveness. The committee met with faculty and staff in that center, concluding the director had done an excellent job and the center was meeting its goals and objectives. So the committee unanimously recommended the director's reappointment.

But not only did the administrator not reappoint the director, he split the center into two parts, demoting the director. When the director appealed to the provost, the latter did not review the matter but informed him this issue was solely within the purview of the research administrator. This disregard by the research administrator of his own process and the reprehensible failure of the provost to act in an oversight capacity for his center speak volumes. Failure of two senior university administrators to perform effectively adds to faculty alienation and does not instill confidence in such administration. Both functioned in a corporate structure where loyalty to fellow administrators had a higher priority than ethics and the best interests of the institution.

Not all ethical matters involve administrators and faculty. In one instance, an undergraduate student asked to carry out a research project under my direction, allowing him to graduate with honors. A senior research associate of mine and I met with the student and discussed a project of limited scope that the student could accomplish part-time over a year. I decided to use my own grant funds to pay for his time in the laboratory. My research colleague oriented

Ethics and the Administrator

him to laboratory procedures, and I volunteered to meet with the student anytime at our mutual convenience. It was his responsibility to plan out his time.

Weeks went by, and no work was done. I called him to my office and inquired as to his continued commitment to an honors thesis. He assured me that though he had other commitments during the academic year, he would spend the summer on the project when he had no classes. During the summer, he came infrequently to the laboratory. I decided not to badger him. One week before graduation, he submitted a report as an honors thesis.

I called him to the office, explaining he had written a report without any experimental work and I would not be party to his fraudulent scheme to graduate with honors. Other students worked hard on their projects, and if his thesis were approved, it would cheapen their efforts. I spent an hour discussing his serious ethical failing. Though bright, achieving a 3.7 cumulative average based on a 4.0 scale, he was trying to cut corners. Perhaps that's how he had functioned, but it would work to his disadvantage when employed. I would do him a disservice by allowing him to succeed in this inappropriate way. I suggested he spend time thinking about whether what he tried to do was ethical.

He was clearly disappointed. I hoped it was salutary, benefiting him in the future. Allan Bloom has aptly stated,[4] "Actually, the family's moral training now comes down to inculcating the bare minimum of social behavior, not lying or stealing, and produce university students who can say nothing more about the ground of their moral action than 'If

Failed Grade

I did that to him, he could do it to me'—an explanation which does not even satisfy those who utter it."

In another instance, a postdoctoral fellow working with me had not been productive but obtained a good position in a pharmaceutical company. As time neared for his departure, he succeeded in contributing to a portion of our program. We jointly agreed he would stay one more month to tie up loose ends. This is not unusual, and I was certain the company would understand. However on the following day, he said he must leave in two weeks. Reluctantly, I agreed but it was clear he would be unable to write up the work for publication. The next day he told me he would be leaving at the end of the week—*two days* notice. Of course, I was furious.

The work he promised could not be accomplished. I told him he was treating me in the most unethical fashion of any associate of mine. It supports my contention that being educated does not guarantee ethical actions. As Allan Bloom said,[5] "...a highly trained computer specialist need not have any more learning about morals, politics, or religion than the most ignorant of persons."

The ethical precepts I used in treating subordinates and superiors will stand any administrator in good stead. As Chester Barnard has said,[6] "The ethical ideal upon which cooperation depends requires the general diffusion of a willingness to subordinate immediate personal interest for both ultimate personal interest and the general good, together with a capacity of individual responsibility."

Before leaving this subject, I think it is relevant to mention the conditions under which an administrator would

Ethics and the Administrator

choose to leave a position. When upper administrators ask one to function unethically in treating faculty, staff, students, alumni, or other administrators; it is time to relinquish the administrative position. The administrator of any organization sets the ethical tone for everyone else, and others respond to those same rules. It is not only what one says that is important but also how one treats others. When integrity, cooperation, and commitment are the exception rather than the norm in any unit, one needs to look no further for the reasons for ethical lapses than the person at the top.

Chapter Fourteen
Recruitment, Retention, and Termination of Colleagues and Subordinates

Recruitment
In a previous chapter, I've discussed in a cursory way recruitment, retention, and termination of associates and subordinates. The processes and individuals selected affect the quality of an administration. It's evident one should attract the best people. The question is how to determine who they are?

Effective recruitment is key to the success of any organization and one of the more important tasks of an academic administrator. There is no formula or set of rules. Neither high academic achievement at graduate school, one's previous title, nor prior experience will guarantee future performance or success. When mediocre administrators talk about aspiring for academic excellence,[1] one should cringe. Many don't appreciate what it is or how

Failed Grade

to attain it, and those institutions where it exists don't discuss it. Excellence involves attracting and retaining the best people. Now, what are their attributes?

Faculty excellence has too often been equated with numbers of external grants an individual has secured. Grants should be a means to an educational end and not an end in itself. However, in the corporate model, the overhead funds generated from these grants are an important objective. In contrast, many faculty members with a strong teaching interest may not generate external funds. Though scholarly research is important, why would any academic administrator retain someone with little interest in teaching?

However, there are increasing numbers of entrepreneurs recruited who are interested solely in their own aggrandizement. According to Rhodes,[2] *"Professionalism has shifted the allegiance of the faculty away from the university.* Consultancy arrangements, company directorships, royalty and patent rights, clients who are wealthy and influential, benefactors bearing gifts, coveys of assistants, generous fees from professional practice, enviable research support, favorable salaries, popular books, successful videotapes, the international lecture circuit, and superior working facilities—these are all typical involvements and enjoyments of the most successful members of the professional faculty. Successful professors view themselves as favoring the university by their presence. It is their base, but scarcely their employer." Their goal is geared to furthering their careers and even in many instances, commercial success. Their objective is

Recruitment, Retention, and Termination of Colleagues and Subordinates

spending less time with students, especially at the undergraduate level, since they aren't useful in the development of the entrepreneur's career.

Some faculty want it both ways: (1) the security and prestige derived from a tenured position at an academic institution, and (2) the benefits of a research institute where research accomplishment is the only important yardstick. To populate academic institutions with such "star" faculty having little interest in teaching or student development does a disservice to students and the institution.

Many universities give lip service to teaching, but in the final analysis faculty members are evaluated and compensated primarily on the grant dollars they bring in. Publications are the basis for justifying additional grants and contracts. The heady feeling of educating students, showing them the excitement of creating new knowledge, is not a corporate priority. If this has little value, why would anyone seek an academic position or why would any administrator retain such a person in a faculty role? Obviously, it's all about money.

We can contrast that attitude with the following. When I called a Nobel Prize-winning colleague to receive an honorary degree at our institution, his very first comment was that his graduate student had recently been awarded the Nobel Prize. Obviously, he was as much delighted with his student's accomplishment as with his own pride in the role he played. Another Nobel Prize recipient insisted on teaching freshman biology at his institution.

So much for the issue that faculty must choose between teaching and scholarship. The two are clearly intertwined

Failed Grade

and both are important at major universities, as they should be. Research must be viewed as a means to an educational objective and not an end in itself. Responsibility for educating the next generation is too important a matter to be relegated to graduate students, research assistants, or staff with little commitment to its accomplishment.

To recruit faculty, one cannot rely only on placing ads in appropriate journals. It is essential to identify faculty members at other institutions for whom one has respect and ask them to identify possible candidates. On one occasion, when recruiting for a specific area, I called an individual for whom I had high regard. One of his former graduate students was completing a postdoctoral fellowship and was looking for a faculty position. He remarked that this person was his best doctoral student and possessed a pleasant personality.

When he came for a seminar, it was apparent that he was the best candidate we had interviewed. He accepted the position and subsequently, it was clear his advisor's recommendation was correct. This faculty member blossomed and was sought by other institutions for faculty and administrative positions. I am reminded of what a colleague once said, "First-class people surround themselves with first-class people; second-class people surround themselves with third-class people."[3] The best available people must be recruited, thereby creating an environment where they will grow and flourish and others will be attracted to the institution.

Administrators have accepted the idea of providing new faculty with financial startup packages so their research

152

Recruitment, Retention, and Termination of Colleagues and Subordinates

programs can begin quickly. This is driven by competition among universities in the amount of external research monies generated. Frequently though, there is little concern with regard to the quality of scholarship, only the money it generates.

Providing support for new faculty is laudatory, but the amount can well exceed several hundred thousands of dollars, especially in the sciences. It's like a signing bonus for a professional athlete. Though new people have financial needs, providing a large, fixed amount to an individual, independent of the academic unit, encourages the view that each person is a separate profit center rather than part of a collegial unit. This environment has bred highly self-oriented, entrepreneurial people in their quest for personal achievement.

Entrepreneurship is instilled at the expense of commitment to teaching, and loyalty to the institution. Academic units are becoming a collection of faculty and not an interdependent and cohesive organization as traditional departments once were. Independent research centers reduce collegiality, adding new complexities where the entrepreneurial professor resembles an independent contractor. Such an environment is not solely due to financial startup packages, but by giving junior people money independent of the unit's needs, senior faculty members can become resentful, feeling no stake in the success of their junior colleagues.

It is relevant to give examples of unsuccessful recruiting. In one case, a new assistant professor was recruited, a person who seemed bright with good communication and

Failed Grade

research skills. But the chair witnessed disquieting signs during the individual's first summer. Instead of developing a research program when he had no teaching responsibilities, the faculty member was away for no apparent reason. His periodic absences continued without satisfactory explanation. When the fall quarter began, he taught the assigned courses. But in the middle of the quarter, he disappeared again. Now students were being unfairly affected.

We discovered this faculty member was experiencing episodes bordering on the psychotic, impairing his ability to function. Pressures in developing courses and an independent research program contributed to his dysfunction. Probing his Ph.D. and postdoctoral advisors, we would have learned there were unexplained absences at those institutions as well. Ultimately, the faculty member left the university and went into industry, where experiencing more structure and less stress, he did an effective job.

In a second case, we were searching for an associate professor who, when recruited, would become the chair of a new division. The selected faculty member had strong support from junior members and from two senior members in the hospital. His poor interpersonal skills only became apparent when he arrived, leading to his ultimate removal as the chair. In his faculty role, he was just a marginal teacher. In scholarship, he had good ideas but lacked follow-through. He was solely "an idea man," and after presenting one idea, he drifted to another. In essence, he was a dilettante. Fortunately, he became bored and left the

Recruitment, Retention, and Termination of Colleagues and Subordinates

university. In recruiting, I failed to use due diligence in determining his strengths and weaknesses at other institutions. Had I probed more effectively, I would have saved us needless grief.

Letters of recommendations have now become useless documents because of the highly litigious environment and the reluctance of people to write candidly and honestly. In these letters, it is not what is said but what is consciously omitted. Talking to individuals on the telephone is a more effective way of gauging a person's potential. An approach I adopted was to call people who had worked with the potential recruit, outline the position and ask pointedly whether they would hire the person. If they hesitated, the answer was obviously no, regardless of what was said. This approach served me well.

Retention

Since recruitment is a key administrative responsibility, it is obvious that retention is of comparable importance. Every administrator should devote a significant amount of time ensuring that the better faculty members are retained.

In one college, there was a junior faculty colleague who appeared to have great potential. A committed teacher, a good researcher, and an excellent collaborator, he was able to compete successfully for grants and to use these resources in educating students. One part of his responsibility during his earlier years was to arrange a seminar program. During one of the lectures involving an individual from outside his department, a senior faculty member in his unit became verbally abusive of the speaker.

Failed Grade

The junior colleague immediately came to the defense of the speaker, but in the process, probably alienated his own senior colleague. Concerned that when his tenure would be considered he might experience retribution, the junior faculty member went to the dean of the college, asking for administrative support for a joint appointment in another unit of the college.

Rather than probing the reasons, the administrator told the faculty member that if he wanted a joint appointment, he should discuss this matter with his chair and that of the other unit. In effect, the administrator disassociated himself from the matter, placing this junior faculty member in the position of making a request of his chair, who might not be supportive. It was the responsibility of the dean to do what he was asking this junior colleague to do. The junior faculty member did not proceed with the joint appointment, but within several years before tenure, he applied for a position at another university and was quickly recruited.

Before he left, the dean made every effort financially to keep him, but it was too late. The seeds for his departure had already been planted. Considering the time and resources spent in recruitment and development, retention of quality junior colleagues should always be an administrative priority.

I've often been puzzled that while colleges are concerned with student retention, even poor ones, there is little concern with faculty turnover. In reviewing administrators for reappointment, an important criterion should be reasons for the departure of quality faculty during that administrator's tenure.

Recruitment, Retention, and Termination of Colleagues and Subordinates

A case in point was the recruitment of a new department chair in a basic science department of another health college. The chair had excellent research credentials and over the ensuing years was successful in securing external support for his research program. However, his dictatorial and arbitrary style as chair alienated the better faculty in his unit. Those able, transferred to other academic units or institutions. By the time he retired sixteen years later, his department had become a shell of its former self. Even though he was apparently destructive in his administrative role, his superiors reappointed him for three additional four-year terms! The administrative competence of those above must be questioned.

Monitoring faculty retention is not only the responsibility of a department chair, a dean, the vice president for academic affairs, and the president, but also the board of trustees. Excellent faculty and administrators are the bedrock of any institution, and their departure may be an early warning sign of administrative incompetence. Superiors should want to probe the reasons. Exit interviews might be a beginning, or calls to those individuals who have left the institution are another way to determine administrative effectiveness. At least, no administrator should be reappointed with a poor track record in retaining better faculty members.

The corporate mentality, instead, looks upon faculty as interchangeable modules. But excellent people are difficult to recruit and not readily replaceable with people of comparable quality. For that reason, barriers should be put in the way of their departure, not a greased slide.

Failed Grade

One of the weaker provosts at one institution became president at two large universities during his career. No one at these institutions inquired of his administrative performance as provost. As president at the second institution, he was responsible for the departure of a very bright faculty member in one of the science departments, who was recruited at the institution where the president had formerly been provost. It was an important coup. One senior faculty member remarked this was the only useful thing the former provost had ever done for the first institution.

In another university, a dean played havoc with the career of a brilliant faculty in one of his departments. The faculty member was very creative and enormously productive with an international reputation and many honors, one being his appointment to a prestigious national academy. On one occasion, he had made a serious error in judgment by apparently "plagiarizing" a small section of the language from another person's grant proposal. The supporting science in his grant however was completely original based upon his own ideas. I do not mean to minimize the gravity of plagiarism and, of course, there must be appropriate punishment. Still, the dean attempted to drive the individual from the university.

The president and the provost of the institution never examined the merits of the case. In their corporate structure, the dean was the final arbiter. A costly, litigious period ensued, and it was only after the dean left the university that cooler and more reasoned heads prevailed and the matter was placed in its proper context.

Recruitment, Retention, and Termination of Colleagues and Subordinates

Where did this vindictive dean go? He became president at another university. The moral of this story is not to be impressed with titles but to judge people based on performance. For an administrator, a key yardstick is the effectiveness in recruiting and retaining better faculty and staff.

Development of Junior Faculty

A key problem at many institutions is the lack of a successful mentoring program for junior faculty. Assuming they should know how to teach and do scholarly activities and that offering advice is an intrusion into their academic freedom is sheer poppycock. Though I learned to be a productive faculty member doesn't mean everyone must learn independently. One can learn effective skills from others. Becoming a good faculty member shouldn't be viewed as a fraternity initiation that, "If I had to do it, everyone should experience the same pain."

Administrators and senior faculty should assist junior colleagues in their development. It must be a structured effort established by the administrator. Attending a junior colleague's lectures, reviewing examinations, and contributing constructive suggestions on grant proposals would demonstrate that their success is important not only for them but for the unit. However, such oversight must not be intrusive. In the final analysis, success or failure of faculty members belongs to them; the role of the administrator is to maximize their chances for success.

Granting tenure is the single most important decision an administrator makes, because of the institution's

Failed Grade

commitment even after the administrator may have departed. The decision must be made considering the best interests of the program, future students, faculty, and administration. Awarding tenure to any individual who is an ineffective teacher or one with little interest in students and teaching is a serious mistake.

Likewise, at major research institutions, it is wrong to grant tenure to questionable researchers who have not established a coherent, scholarly program during their probationary periods. Laymen have often asked why scholarship is important at a university. If a person is a good teacher, isn't that sufficient? Probably the best lecturer I've heard was an individual who was dynamic, well-organized, and retained students' attention with humor and examples, but his material was twenty years old and no longer relevant. A person engaged in research would not have given a lecture without reviewing the current literature. I believe that research has made me a better teacher, acquainting me with new knowledge and up-to-date examples for lectures.

In evaluating colleagues during a probationary period, it is important that each person has an annual written review, identifying strengths, areas needing improvement and what are future expectations. This is not the sole responsibility of the administrator but it must include faculty members above the rank of the individual being considered for tenure and promotion.

Recruitment, Retention, and Termination of Colleagues and Subordinates

Termination

Even under ideal conditions, there are times when individuals should not be awarded tenure but need to be terminated. Obviously, that person should be treated fairly and with respect. If due process is not adhered to, the result can cause anguish for everyone concerned.

For example, an administrator told a junior faculty member he was doing a satisfactory job. However, there were strong indications his didactic courses were substandard. Good students had complained. None of the senior faculty had attended his lectures, and the chair did so infrequently. When his dossier was reviewed by the tenure and promotion committee and the student evaluation of teaching forms were considered, it was apparent he was a weak teacher without improving during the probationary period. He was denied tenure. But, by not informing him earlier and in writing, the administrator had done him a disservice. In that way, he could have found a more suitable position sooner and not be under the illusion he would be granted tenure.

My philosophy on tenure has been, if in doubt, say no because in the long term inadequate faculty set lower standards for the next generation of students and colleagues. There are cases where capable people were denied tenure at one institution and had distinguished careers at another. I remember one assistant professor inquired of me as to how many publications he would need to be granted tenure. It was a ridiculous query.

The quality of research should not be based on numbers of publications or grants awarded. We have gone down that

Failed Grade

slippery slope, relying on quantitative data as a substitute for reasoned professional judgments. We have placed too much importance on what governmental agencies think is good research. They should not be the final arbiters. One faculty member implied that the National Institutes of Health was his boss. He was not being disrespectful, but was simply stating the importance in generating external funding to support his students.

But today's seemingly important research may be unimportant tomorrow. Similarly, those proposals out of favor today might be important ones tomorrow. Research was obviously of great importance to Albert Einstein, one of the scientific giants of the twentieth century. But he said later in his life, "It is the supreme art of the teacher to awaken joy in creative expression and knowledge." That statement remains what education is all about.

To assess faculty teaching, peer evaluation is more reliable than that of students. Peers are educational professionals; students are neophytes who may not have sufficient appreciation of quality education. Currying students' favor by setting low standards and giving high grades may result in better scores in the students' evaluation of the teaching, but no one benefits from an environment of low academic standards, least of all students and the institution's reputation.

There exists rigidity in many colleges and universities in the tenure process. Frequently, little is done before the time for decision unless the candidate has performed egregiously. If a junior faculty is performing in a superior way and merits tenure, a long delay is unnecessary. On the

Recruitment, Retention, and Termination of Colleagues and Subordinates

other hand also, when the candidate is inadequate, why wait? The humane thing is to terminate the faculty member when it is evident retention will not occur.

The quality of staff too must be vigorously assessed. By retaining people who are incompetent, more work is generated for others. Their termination must occur to preserve resources and create a better working environment, especially since finances in academia are clearly limited.

A painful example confronted me when I inherited an administrator with a disabled husband. She was pleasant and affable but incompetent. Her budgets were never submitted on time, yet she talked for hours with the janitor. She played favorites among faculty and staff reporting to her with no vision of the future. Her position was not tenured, and the upper administration and I agreed her association with the university should be ended. I agonized until the day I called her into my office to inform her of the decision. She was given seven months, which seemed a reasonable length of time to find a new position. It was the correct decision, difficult as it was for me personally.

A major role for administrators is dealing with such difficult decisions and arriving at one that is fair to all concerned. Consideration of legal suits and other factors must not inhibit one's actions. As President Harry Truman remarked, "If you can't stand the heat, get out of the kitchen."

Failed Grade

Collegiality

Before concluding this chapter, some thoughts on collegiality are appropriate. The issues of quality teaching, superior research, and excellent service may be amenable to some objectivity. Too often in the past, collegiality has been highly subjective and used to discriminate against women and those of different religions, races, and ethnic origins. Academic institutions must demonstrate complete objectivity and lack of bias.

Just as negative and disruptive people are not tolerated in corporations, likewise, they should not populate academia. Such individuals are attracted to academia because many are bright, articulate, and once granted tenure, they appear impossible to remove. Yet, students and academic colleagues bear the brunt of their negativism and dysfunctional behavior.

At an Ivy League school, two faculty members in a science department had so much antagonism toward each other that not only did they not communicate, but they also forbade graduate students from discussing research with those directed by the other person. Such a non-collegial environment should never be tolerated, regardless of how acclaimed these individuals were. At another institution, I observed a highly dysfunctional person placed in a department of one to minimize his negative effects on colleagues. Obviously, he shouldn't have been granted tenure.

I look forward to the time when people in this multicultural society will be treated and valued as individuals. And those with antisocial behavior will not

Recruitment, Retention, and Termination of Colleagues and Subordinates

merely be isolated, but will no longer be welcomed into academia. It will take time, but it will occur when the corrosive effect such people have on colleagues and the learning environment of students is realized.

Chapter Fifteen
Environment Creation, Decision Making, and Problem Solving

Environment Creators

Probably the single most important function of an administrator is as environment creator for everyone. That individual sets the agenda, the issues to be dealt with, how the budget is used, and the tone and the ambience for the unit.

The corporate structure suits some administrators especially, providing an ideal opportunity to achieve their own personal objectives with little attention to creating an effective environment. In essence, some people seek administrative positions because of what the unit or institution and its budget can do for them, rather than as a service to others. Some thrive on controlling the environment of others, and the selection process unfortunately has often been geared to those wanting the

Failed Grade

position and not those who possess the attributes needed for administrative success.

Weak administrators are basically of two types. One is oblivious to the administrator's role as an environment creator. This person believes if he or she can be an administrator, then anybody can. Therefore no one person is better than another in the organization and people are expendable and interchangeable.

For example, once, when approached by another university to apply for a comparable administrative position, I decided to do so. The position was offered, but for personal reasons I was not anxious to leave the area. Before making a final decision, I decided to meet with the university's president where I currently worked to determine his interest in keeping me.

My relationship with him had been a reasonable one. During my tenure, enrollment had increased, the quality of faculty and staff had improved, and we were reaching out to alumni and industry for external support. When I told him I had been offered the position at another institution, he looked at me and, without even asking me to stay, said, "Al, that is a very good university. Who can take over for you here?"

In effect, my leaving had become a greased slide. It wasn't that he wanted me to leave; he felt one administrator was as good as another, that many could have done my job. After they recruited my replacement, however, there was turmoil since my successor had difficulty relating to the better faculty in the unit.

Environment Creation, Decision Making, and Problem Solving

A second type of poor environment creator is a person who is either insecure, requiring unswerving fealty by others, or is domineering and vindictive. In any case, an unproductive environment results. I recall a bright, honest, and highly creative associate to a newly recruited senior administrator. The two did not get along from the outset, and the associate was encouraged to leave his administrative position and return to the faculty ranks where he was successful in teaching, research, and in the recruitment of excellent junior colleagues. However his very presence was a continual source of irritation, and when an opportunity arose, the administrator transferred him to a unit outside the college with alacrity. Ultimately, the person left the university. The result was that his particular expertise was greatly diminished in the college since the better junior faculty left the university as well.

Obviously, there are examples of administrators improving their environment. In one case, an administrator had recently assumed his position, and a faculty member, who had accepted a position at another university, wanted to meet with him to explain his reasons for leaving. The administrator invited the faculty member to his home and listened attentively to the problems the faculty member encountered. His reasons for leaving were understandable. But the administrator realized he didn't want to lose him. As they parted amicably, the administrator said he appreciated the commitment he had made but was interested in having him return when the environment was more supportive. Within two years, the faculty member came back and proved highly productive.

Failed Grade

In another instance, an administrative assistant decided to leave shortly after the arrival of a new administrator. To find her replacement, the administrator examined the credentials of various applicants. Two were selected for personal interviews. Since a number of secretaries would be reporting to this person, the administrator felt it appropriate each secretary interview the two candidates and make recommendations. Though many secretaries felt the internal person was preferable, the administrator selected the outside candidate. At the conclusion, many secretaries sent notes thanking the administrator for asking their opinions. In effect, he gave them dignity. They were not merely appendages to the organization but people whose counsel was appreciated. The inclusive environment where advice was sought was welcomed, regardless of the final choice.

Although people gravitate to academia for other than financial reasons, merit and salary increases generally are a key part in creating a productive environment. One faculty member I remember was highly productive but difficult to deal with. After reviewing his accomplishments, I felt it appropriate he receive the largest increment. I did not allow personal feelings to interfere with objective evaluation. By contrast, there was one dean who received a salary percentage less than the maximum permitted by the institution. Outraged at upper administration, he said no one in his unit would get a higher percentage than he. In effect, everyone was to be penalized because of his pique.

Attempting to satisfy the best people does not imply one should kowtow to unjustified demands. In one case, the

Environment Creation, Decision Making, and Problem Solving

chair of a unit involved in an interdisciplinary program and another colleague outside his unit agreed that this program should be expanded. I agreed and felt a third faculty member should be recruited to another unit, bringing different expertise into the program. But the chair was adamant, wanting any new faculty member added to his division alone. I listened respectfully but discerned no rational justification. We recruited an excellent person but since he was not placed in his division, I gained the chair's enmity. However, I would not allow myself to be manipulated. An administrator doesn't have the luxury of allowing personal irritations to color one's relationships. Acquiescing to unsupported demands, however, demonstrates a lack of leadership.

An administrator's role is to establish an environment where individuals can achieve their goals and objectives. However, it is essential for the administrator to expect individuals in the group to contribute to the unit's development. Faculty members are not free agents, but important players in a cohesive organization, each having a responsibility to assist in the creation of a productive environment. It is not necessary that people like one another but essential that there be civility in public discourse leading to decisions.

An academic environment must also have an open and intellectually challenging atmosphere, receptive to many diverse opinions. An administrator's role is to ensure civility and toleration of such views. Growth and development of faculty and staff can only be assured by their active participation in decision making. This is

171

Failed Grade

important not just for their development but also for the entire system.

Administrative Vision

Administrators must have vision, creativity, and time to address problems. This responsibility cannot be delegated to others.[2] One role of the administrator is to anticipate future changes, and persuade others by the cogency of arguments as to those directions. It is necessary for the administrator to be proactive and not reactive. The future is murky, and situations always arise that might not have been anticipated. This process is ongoing, not an episodic one.

Time, above all, is a limiting resource for administrators and must be viewed as a zero-sum game. If matters can be delegated but are handled by the administrator, less time can be devoted to issues that no one else can address. Identifying those matters is a high priority. Being nimble is not as important as being correct, and if longer time is required, so be it. Addressing problems should be a high priority, but that doesn't mean planning and implementation are solely administrative prerogatives. It is necessary to share the processes with faculty and staff. Only then do such plans become commitments of the entire unit, though timing and sequence of events remain with the administrator.

Process in Decision Making

Frequently administrators in their haste want people on a committee who will support their views. This creates the perception that conclusions have already been

Environment Creation, Decision Making, and Problem Solving

predetermined, and the committee is being used as a proverbial fig leaf, not a deliberative body. There is always tension and, at times, frank distrust by faculty of administrative intentions. However, the administrator's responsibility is to ameliorate such attitudes and create an environment where faculty and administrators work in harmony.

For this reason, it is desirable to include on committees people not always favorably disposed to the views of the administrator. Though their opinions may ultimately be modified, a thoughtful and reasoned conclusion may evolve upon examining the matters in depth. But even if that doesn't occur, it is preferable to have these individuals part of the deliberative process than outside it. If the majority view is not theirs, there can be no criticism that the committee engaged in a "railroad" process. Perceptions can be as important as reality.

Some administrators are clearly impatient, and others are dilatory to the extreme. All of the above are wrong. Administrators don't have the right to force ideas on all, as in a corporate, "top-down" structure. But they do have a right to express possible goals and objectives and ask faculty and staff to consider these in a reasonable time frame. The timeline for a decision is the prerogative of administrators but not the conclusions of others.

Administrative Planning

The term "long-range planning" has crept into the modern lexicon of academic administrators. It was purloined from industry and viewed as an essential

Failed Grade

component in academic planning. But planning must be an ongoing part of any administrative unit, and the distinction between short-range and long-range planning is strictly artificial. A new administrator should examine the entire faculty, the staff, the academic programs, the student body, the facilities/infrastructure, and the budget.

First, what are the faculty strengths and weaknesses and how can the former be maximized? This is both short-range and long-range planning; the two are interconnected. Similarly, is the staffing appropriate and are the individual roles well defined? Can the number on the administrative staff be pared down without affecting efficiency? This is an important matter every administrator should consider, even though addressing it may require a much longer time frame and the attrition of some existing personnel.

Unfortunately in a corporate structure, reducing administrative size is rarely considered as a means for improving efficiency and decreasing costs. What changes in existing academic programs should be contemplated, which are marginal and should be ultimately terminated, and which new programs should be considered? How can student quality be enhanced? Are facilities and infrastructure adequate to meet anticipated changes in the next five to ten years? If not, what processes must be initiated?

As noted, the process can be as important as the decision. Is the budget adequate to carry out desired changes? The administrator's responsibility is to maximize the existing budget and prioritize what can be accomplished within its limits.

Environment Creation, Decision Making, and Problem Solving

Once when interviewing for a senior administrative position, I saw a glaring problem that needed to be addressed. Over time, I came to the reluctant conclusion that a key person in the hospital was inhibiting our academic program. He had to be removed from his administrative position. I began the process by sensitizing my superiors. It took me six years to accomplish this result because of continual changes in administrators above me.

What I realized is that one must approach such unpleasant tasks without any vindictiveness but with commitment, pleasantness, and great persistence. One doesn't have the luxury of becoming impatient and irritable. Planning and justification are the key elements to achieve important and worthwhile objectives.

In another instance, I was involved with the dean of another college in developing a new connecting building that would house faculty from both colleges. At the time, it seemed justified based upon space pressures. However, before the building was constructed and occupied, an early-retirement program was instituted. A number of senior faculty members retired from both colleges and were not replaced. This led to a reduction in space pressures. It was an ideal time for the university to examine the optimal use of the new laboratory-designed science building.

Obviously, some space could be used for the two colleges, but it could serve other important purposes. Such a priority was the status of the biochemistry program. There were, in effect, three biochemistry programs in three different colleges and some biochemical-oriented faculty in two other colleges. At varying times, the university had

175

Failed Grade

brought these faculty members together to discuss the future of biochemistry. It was an important question since one could expect a superb program with all the resources that were being spent. However, since these were distributed in at least three colleges, they were not used optimally. But planning on what should happen to the biochemistry program was the responsibility of the office of academic affairs and not the individual colleges where parts of the program resided.

Feeble attempts were made to create a single graduate program developed around courses currently offered. The important question was not presented in the right context, namely, should there be a single biochemistry program? If the answer were yes, then it became the responsibility of academic affairs to implement that decision. It is impossible to have a cohesive faculty spread throughout campus. By using part of the new laboratory building to house all biochemical faculty members, the basis for a single department would be at hand. The question of who would chair this unit and in which college it would be housed had been postponed to the last, as it should be.

By insisting all biochemistry courses, regardless of what they were called, would be the responsibility of this new department, one would be creating an environment with a reduction in duplication and maximizing the use of financial resources. Ultimately, there might be fewer faculty required, and those recruited would meet existing deficiencies. For the first time, there would be a single entity with the focus of creating a high-quality and cohesive program. At that point, addressing which college

Environment Creation, Decision Making, and Problem Solving

the program would be housed in and how the chair would be selected are appropriate questions. This issue demonstrates that process and sequence of events are important in achieving the objectives. Without adequate planning, the desired goals are not attained.

Other Problem-Solving Matters

Not all environment creation and problem-solving issues have pure motives. Sometimes politics, control, and power can be the real motivating factors.

There was an individual who had a very senior administrative position and had contributed significantly to the university. A new president was selected, and tension immediately arose between these two individuals, culminating in the elimination of the administrative position of the president's adversary. After many years of doing a creditable job in administration, this was a grievous blow to the senior administrator and adversely affected the rest of his academic career.

All of the above examples illustrate the involvement of administrators in environment creation, decision making, and problem solving; all three are intertwined. Planning is an ongoing, not an episodic process. The administrator must determine which matters should be addressed, their priority, and create a suitable environment where these can be dealt with effectively. The administrator should bring together those impacted, solicit their views, and set time parameters for the issues to be considered. There should be greater transparency in the planning process to ensure longevity of one's actions.

177

Failed Grade

However, in the evolving corporate structure, there is even less meaningful interplay between administrators, faculty, and staff than in the collegial model. Virtually all decisions in a "top-down" structure originate and are implemented by administration. But multiple inputs and shared governance produce more reasoned decisions with the potential for greater longevity and value to the institution.

Chapter Sixteen
Maximizing the Contributions of Associates

In addition to recruiting people and creating a supportive environment for them, a major responsibility of the administrator is maximizing the contributions of the staff. Of all the chapters in this book, this one is more generic and applies to any organization.

As with the recruitment of faculty, the selection of administrative associates is of great importance and speaks volumes as to the kind of administrator one is. Does one select obsequious types who shower the administrator with superlatives trying to determine what they perceive he or she will want to hear? Or does one choose honest, forthright people with minds of their own, telling the administrator what he or she may not want to hear?

The responsibilities of staff and other associates are those delegated to them by the administrator. Their role shouldn't be designed solely for meeting the needs of the

Failed Grade

administrator. The goal of any administrative structure is to facilitate the contributions of others. And the function of the top administrator is to transmit that responsibility to associates and obtain their commitment to achieve such objectives.

At the outset, any administrator has significant latitude in selecting associates. If the administrative structure increases, it does so at the expense of other needs of the unit since resources are a zero sum game. For this reason an administrator's duty is to make the administrative structure as lean as possible. In the corporate university environment this isn't the case. Administrators have become detached from the needs, activities, and priorities of faculty and staff and often insulate themselves with personnel who contribute to administrative bloat. They use the new golden rule, "Whoever controls the gold makes the rules" including the number of assistants/associates needed.

Twenty years ago, organizations were able to function effectively with half the number of today's administrative staff, and they undoubtedly functioned more efficiently. The role of the administrator is to examine the personnel structure inherited and determine whether contraction by eliminating single-issue staff and using those with multiple functions would be desirable.

Staff should have distinct, well-defined roles necessary in meeting the organization's objectives. By identifying those responsibilities, everyone in the unit knows what these are. Tying responsibilities with authority demonstrates an administrator's confidence in the assistant and provides clear lines of authority for others to

Maximizing the Contributions of Associates

understand and use. Rarely are other constituencies asked to evaluate the performance of various administrative assistants. Such evaluation would permit the senior administrator, with input from those being served, to evaluate the staff person's performance and effectiveness.

One problem is confidentiality. People are reluctant to be critical of anyone in the administrative organization, knowing they may be dependent upon that individual for activities that will affect them. The senior administrator should be sensitive to that issue and have little interest in knowing who provides the evaluation but should want to know the effectiveness of the assistant in meeting the needs of others in the organization. It is clear if the administrator is unhappy with an assistant that person will be removed. However, if the assistant were incompetent in serving the needs of others, that person should be terminated as well.

An instance of some of the issues involving associate staff occurred when I assumed my second major administrative position. I requested additional resources for a budget officer. My predecessor was an excellent administrator performing all aspects related to the unit's budget. I realized I could do that but felt my time could be better spent relating to various constituencies and creating an endowment.

The university approved my request, and we were fortunate in recruiting an excellent person with high integrity. He kept me fully apprised of our financial status. When we had yearly budget meetings with the university's administration, he was always prepared. The material assembled and the report provided reflected well, not only

181

Failed Grade

on him but our administration. He needed little direction and oversight. As a consequence, he had great latitude and rewarded the organization with sterling performances. Though he held a subordinate position in my administration, he was working for the best interests of the college and not only mine. His responsibilities were to the institution.

I expected occasionally he would make mistakes, but those times were very rare. In those instances, we discussed the matter and what may have been a preferable course of action privately as colleagues. It was important for both of us to learn from mistakes and for me to show respect for the job he was doing. He gained the respect of the senior faculty and staff, and people went directly to him to solve problems. He had responsibility and authority, and people knew I would support his decisions. This appointment benefited me and the college, freeing me to devote time to matters others would have been incapable of doing.

Time is a finite resource for every administrator. As Peter Drucker has said, "Time is the scarcest resource, and unless it is managed, nothing else can be managed."[1] One's associates are partners in this endeavor. I knew one dean who involved himself in every single issue in his college, some of which should have been handled by others. The development of his associates was stunted, but more importantly, he didn't have time to focus on issues that only he could have addressed.

My brother, who spent the major part of his professional life in industry, viewed the administrator as a coach. It is an apt term. I wanted administrative subordinates to develop

182

Maximizing the Contributions of Associates

and assume positions with greater responsibilities in the future. I was their mentor. I showed them the way I approached problems. It isn't that my way was the best way; it was *a* way. In the course of time, they would arrive at their own judgments as to which approaches were good ones. In essence, I viewed these subordinates as students whose role was to learn to become better administrators.

Administration is not a spectator sport, for experiences mold one's development. I shared with these subordinates the problems I was dealing with. We met as a group each week for not more than two hours. As Peter Drucker has advised,[2] "As a rule, meetings should never be allowed to become the main demand on an executive's time." The meetings were informal but confidential. I wanted sensitive issues raised and kept within the confines of the meeting. Gossiping outside the meeting was not tolerated since it inhibited an honest exchange of ideas.

In these give-and-take dialogues no one dominated the discussion. They served several purposes: (1) that administration was not simply a collection of people but a cohesive and interactive unit; (2) that each person was expected to contribute and not be merely a passive listener; and (3) that all opinions were valued whether or not I or others agreed with those conclusions.

Unfortunately, university meetings for deans did not have that format except in rare instances. They were informational, provided by the staff of the vice president for academic affairs, and this information could have been relayed by campus mail, not wasting the collective time of all. Perhaps with e-mail, this is being done now.

183

Failed Grade

Apparently, there was a lack of trust that meetings devoted to problems would remain confidential. At any rate, I was rarely used by upper administration for this purpose. I was not offended, since I was busy coping with my own problems and had no need to offer advice at the university level. However, I felt presidents and provosts were the losers because they could have benefited from the ideas and opinions of other deans.

As an administrator, I preferred to hear of problems first. When told by someone they had good news and bad news, I always wanted the bad news first. My subordinates knew I wanted to be the first apprised of serious problems, since my role was to develop strategies to cope with them. I was never irritated with those who brought me bad news. They were doing their job, and mine was to help solve these problems. Of course, one learns of successes in due time, but the difficult problems are what an administrator must address first. One of the greater U.S. presidents, Harry Truman, said "The buck stops here." Successes and failures in problem resolution begin at the top.

Another role for the administrator is becoming an effective cheerleader. The administrator should be optimistic, viewing the future in positive terms. Successes of the unit are not to be arrogated to the administrator but distributed to the colleagues responsible for that accomplishment. They should be acknowledged orally to others and in written form to the individual, thereby reducing administrative turnover. Financial remuneration is generally not the major factor in attrition. Appreciation and recognition by one's bosses and peers is probably at least as

Maximizing the Contributions of Associates

important. I distributed the successes and claimed the failures.

It is inappropriate to castigate a subordinate in public and probably in private as well for any failure. A more germane question is what happened, and who, if anyone, was responsible? Honest answers to straightforward questions. The subordinate needs to know he or she will not be raked over the coals. It is more important to find out what happened. Was supervision by the administrator in charge lax? Did he or she allow the person too much latitude and that ineffective communication between them resulted in poor decisions? I tried never to be harsh with someone who had made an honest mistake, but I was very unhappy with any attempted cover-up. I wanted people to be forthright with me as I was with them.

Finally, the environment that has caused problems for staff and related associates without faculty titles should be addressed. The corporate structure has added to the difficulties that some experience. It is essential that staff remuneration be based on performance, and not arbitrarily limited by job classification.

When a member of the staff reaches a salary ceiling in their category so that they can expect only cost-of-living increases in the future, job dissatisfaction and staff turnover can be expected. Loss of good people places an additional burden on administration since turnover generates unnecessary costs in training new people. The time devoted to other initiatives is reduced.

A title should describe what the person does. Everybody does not need to be an administrative assistant when

Failed Grade

functioning largely in a secretarial capacity. There is nothing menial or demeaning in such important activities. Yet through salary limitations, the present environment has spawned "title-inflation." This results from attempts to obviate the restrictive effect of job classification by calling many people administrative assistants and thereby obfuscating their actual function. For this reason the system of rigid job classifications should be discussed widely before being implemented. At some future time, perhaps we'll return to a more sensible, less restrictive environment allowing merit increases based solely on a person's performance. Playing games to reward valuable associates is a degrading activity with a time cost.

The Hippocratic Oath, "Do no harm," should apply not only to physicians but also to administrators and their associates. In fact it should be part of every administrator's creed. That doesn't mean one should maintain the status quo—far from it. Administration clearly requires creativity, but it must be reasoned and carefully considered since the success of every organization depends directly on the effectiveness of its administration.

Chapter Seventeen
Administrative Compensation, Financial
Decision Making, and Budget Utilization

Administrative Compensation

Nowhere is it more apparent that institutions of higher education have become a corporate structure than by examining administrative compensation and the rhetoric for its rationale. The differential between senior faculty and administration increased remarkably during the 1990s with little discussion as to its impact on collegiality and its portent for the future. Derek Bok, former president at Harvard University, argued several years ago for CEO levels of pay for university presidents.

In the November 24, 2000, issue of *The Chronicle of Higher Education*, the salaries and benefits earned by presidents in seventy-four private colleges in 1998-99 were reported. Ms. Couger, president-elect of the College and University Professional Association for Human Resources,

Failed Grade

enunciated the justification for these large salaries. She stated, "The boards of trustees are seeing these individuals (presidents) as comparable to CEOs of corporations and are beginning to compensate them accordingly."

In the August 30, 2002, issue of *The Chronicle of Higher Education,* Julianne Basinger and Seth Perry[1] have authored a special report on the financial compensation of presidents of public universities. In both instances, we are witnessing the creation of the imperial presidency, not only with university housing, but cars with drivers, home assistance personnel, separate travel budgets, and significant "deferred compensation packages." The analogy with CEOs in corporations is striking. It's not surprising since boards of colleges and universities are composed principally of men and women from the corporate sector.

The argument is made, without any supportive evidence, that it is difficult to attract good people to these positions. And moreover, the role of the president has changed. The president has become the public relations and marketing person, a fundraiser and a politician. Nowhere is it questioned: Are these activities important ones for a university president and senior administrators?

Presidents' role as academicians has clearly a lower priority. For these multiple roles, the argument goes, they should be appropriately compensated. The real reason, however, for these exorbitant salaries is that just as CEOs in corporations control their boards of directors, determining who is on compensation committees, so too university presidents now have a strong say in what issues

Administrative Compensation, Financial Decision Making, and Budget Utilization

the boards of trustees address and politic overtly or covertly for their own compensation package.

Salary differentials between top academic administrators and most senior faculty are now approaching a factor of ten. And that relates only to the institution's direct compensation, excluding housing, cars, travel, entertainment budget, and "deferred compensation" that presidents receive. Not taken into account is compensation generated by serving on corporate boards and foundations or the lecture circuit, activities arising from the individual's university position.

In corporations, pay increases for CEOs in fifty major companies increased by 866 percent since 1985 versus a 63 percent increase for the average worker in those companies.[2] Similarly, salaries and total compensation of university presidents are increasing rapidly when compared with faculty and staff, and some are approaching seven figures annually. This is an indication of the corporate environment in today's university. At an earlier time, the salary of a president at one major public university could not exceed that of the state's governor.[3]

In turn, presidents select other administrators, vice presidents, provosts, and deans whose compensation is frequently based on the size of their budgets. This significant differential has generated an administrative class and a faculty/staff class. A "we and they" relationship produces greater tension, a less collegial environment, and increased polarization between administration and faculty. In the past, administrators were drawn from senior faculty who understood higher education and functioned for a

189

Failed Grade

limited time period in administration before returning to the faculty.

Financial Allocations

At one time, administrative costs collectively were a small part of the total academic budget.[4] The huge increase arises partly from increased administrative staff, personnel dealing with federal and state mandates, development activities, legal issues, relationships with corporations, and contact with research agencies in Washington. Governmental regulations at federal and state levels and increases in formalized university procedures and record keeping have contributed as well. Many are un-funded mandates and the byproduct of political intrusion into academic institutions.

New programs designed to redress discrimination with diversity and other past grievances might not contribute to increased costs, but appointment of "single-issue" administrators and staff to monitor their effectiveness does. Thereby senior administrators are protected from criticism through public relations support.

The environment in the past was at best neutral to all students. Student failure and costs associated with attrition were of little consequence. Now institutions offer remedial courses[5] to those unprepared for college. Obviously, significant costs, not addressed previously, must be met.

Also, equal opportunity legislation has affected athletic and all sport programs. Facilities for women's athletic offerings must now be provided. While these costs may be borne by the athletic department, they affect the

Administrative Compensation, Financial Decision Making, and Budget Utilization

university's administration, facilities, and personnel. Related is the concern of journalists and politicians with graduation rates of student athletes. Finances, in the public relations arena, are used to justify commitment to students. Student retention has become of importance to the academic administrator, and resources must be allocated for that activity.

Disabled students in the past had to contend with an unsympathetic environment at colleges and universities. With the Americans with Disabilities Act, that attitude has changed. Facilities have been modified and staff hired. Professors have become sensitized to such needs. As a consequence, new administrative costs have been required.

The current litigious environment is also influencing colleges and universities financially. Students, faculty, and staff, feeling unfairly treated on almost any issue, seek redress in the courts and by unionization. Whether or not successful, the institution has to defend itself. Legal expenses have increased appreciably and lawyers added to the staff to counsel institutional administration in grievances and in preparing legal documents and contracts. Considerable litigation costs have now become a part of the academic landscape.

Other costs involve the hiring of law-enforcement personnel to create a safe environment for everyone. In the past, academic institutions were largely isolated from criminal activity in the general society, but no longer. On another safety matter, the Occupational Safety and Health Authority (OSHA) and the Nuclear Regulatory Agency have responsibility for ensuring safe practices are used in

Failed Grade

institutions. Potentially dangerous activities once tolerated in laboratories or in clinical settings are now monitored by college/university personnel to ensure that governmental regulations are adhered to. Obviously, costs are associated with these activities.

With the hiring of entrepreneurial faculty and staff and the desire to patent new discoveries, universities added staff to deal with such matters. Companies in the corporate sector may want to license these inventions and bring potential products to market. They must be contacted. All these activities add to administrative expenses.

Factors contributing to increased administrative costs and a finite budget have prompted senior administrators to ask colleges to justify their budgets, and with rising costs, administration has not only increased tuition but has looked to academic programs to recoup monies for expanding administrative needs. While some may be necessary, they all should be examined in terms of their importance to student education. Can some of them be pared or eliminated?

In my experience at almost every budgeting cycle, new terms were used with the same objective in mind to wring from academic programs resources for new initiatives and administrative positions. Terms such as "reallocation, redistribution, recision, readjustment, reduction, rebasing," etc., not to mention "reserves," were designed for achieving this objective. One dean rightly said these "re-" words were the bane of his existence.

*Administrative Compensation, Financial Decision Making,
and Budget Utilization*

Budget Utilization and Programs as Profit Centers

In a similar budgetary game, one president encouraged all deans to spend down residual balances in their accounts to justify the annual budget the university was receiving from state government. Said he to the deans, "Spend down your balances. I'll be your banker." But there was one problem that deans realized in retrospect. When that president left his position, the new incumbent had no commitment to such prior fiscal arrangements. In a related vein, one dean spent his residual budget wildly two months before the beginning of the next fiscal year. He feared he must use it or lose it, and if the full budget weren't expended, how could he justify the same budget for the following year?

The concept of depleting resources to justify the budget for the next year is fallacious. There may be cogent reasons to carry forward balances. Such balances may be used for purchasing major pieces of capital equipment, the replacement and maintenance of computers and existing equipment, and for startup costs for new faculty. And, of course, there are unforeseen emergencies that cannot be anticipated at budget time. Allowing balances to be carried forward may be wise fiscally. It demonstrates confidence the administrator will spend these resources prudently at some future time.

A byproduct of the corporate mentality is to view every academic program as a profit center. After contributing to the university's administrative costs, each is a vessel sitting on its own "bottom." No longer is the institution a collegial environment of various programs with competing demands,

Failed Grade

differing interdependencies and needs, and various cost structures, but it is viewed as a collection of corporate units. The senior administrator tries to demonstrate fairness and be insulated from criticism.[6] By doing so, the institution is moving on the path to autopilot. In that scenario, the computer takes over determining the appropriate budget for each. As Henry Rosovsky said appropriately,[7] "A university cannot be run by cost accountants or as a commercial enterprise responding only to changing markets. That is bad for us and worse for the societies we seek to serve."

A budget traditionally allocated to an academic unit becomes the responsibility of the administrator in charge. Since 90 percent or more of that budget is for personnel costs, only a small fraction is for discretionary purposes. Needed supplies and maintenance of equipment reduces the discretionary amount of money available.

One of the more pernicious abuses of some administrators is travel. Administrators, accountable only to themselves, may travel more extensively than they should, whereas this would not be permitted of faculty. As dean, I felt I was custodian of the college's budget, and the job was to maximize its use for the benefit of everyone. In many instances, it was preferable to send faculty to professional meetings where they'd be exposed to the latest information benefiting students than my taking a trip of marginal importance to the institution. My approach was to ask how I would want the travel budget expended if I were a faculty member or a member of the upper administration. As with every decision, the issue is one of fairness to the unit. Too

Administrative Compensation, Financial Decision Making, and Budget Utilization

much administrative travel creates a need for more staff to act during the administrator's absences. The failure to monitor such travel shows a lack of administrative oversight.

My single most difficult administrative decision was allocating salary raises for faculty and staff from the annual budget pool. How should each person's contribution be recognized while not thwarting the motivation of those who had not been productive that year but were still trying? Creating a positive environment was important. If one individual received a significant increase and another received zero, there would be animosity by the latter, not only to the individual receiving the larger amount but also toward the unit itself. My responsibility was the judicious distribution of increments, mitigating dissatisfaction of those receiving the lowest increases and maximizing satisfaction of the productive and more mobile faculty. I never gave a zero percent increase.

For junior faculty and staff, each was concerned with the total amount of the salary raise. Senior personnel were more concerned with the percentage increase since the institution reported that average percentage. In effect, it was a "no-win" situation. I agonized over annual increments as small as $120, trying to prevent personal likes or dislikes from affecting my decision.

There should be objective criteria for increases. Consequently, each faculty was asked to prepare a brief activity statement for the preceding year. I didn't want the process to be time consuming but wanted the information to assist me, with advice from the chairs of their units, in

Failed Grade

faculty evaluation. By inference, each year was a new beginning. Needless to say, there are many intangibles, and the activity statement was merely one component in assessing an individual's contribution.

Such documents have been expanded for the purpose of managerial accounting, a pernicious byproduct of the business world. One cardinal rule is not to base decisions on personal relationships or an individual's aggressiveness. Impartiality and fair-mindedness are the hallmarks of a good academic administrator, and these can be ascertained in the allocation of salary increases.

Difficulties involving salary issues stem from the pressure of some aggressive and productive faculty who want special treatment. A faculty member once called me from a professional meeting and asked for a salary increase in the middle of the academic year. The message was another institution was interested and if the increase were not forthcoming, the faculty member would consider leaving.

I responded that I needed time to consider the request and its implications. After reflection, I informed the person I was unprepared to change existing precedents but would consider the request at the next annual salary increase. What is fair for one should be fair for all. If exceptions are made, a chaotic environment can result, and retaining any one person is not worth that result. Incidentally, the person did not leave the college but learned such pressure tactics would not work with me.

However, there are university administrators who are not guided by fairness. In one instance, faculty salaries were

Administrative Compensation, Financial Decision Making, and Budget Utilization

frozen because of a poor state economy, but members of so-called "revenue-generating units" were given decent salary increments silently and without public knowledge. When that information became known, it damaged the credibility of the entire administration.

Not all budget decisions involve salary matters. Allocating money for travel and equipment are important issues as well. One should be guided by appropriate justification. One method was to establish small faculty committees, composed of individuals with no vested interest. These committees functioned in an advisory and not a decision-making capacity since I did not want to be excluded from this process but to gain the wisdom of others before making the decisions. These procedures were useful in allocating travel funds and in new equipment purchases. The advantage is all requests are considered equally with no back channels for receiving special treatment.

Since discretionary funds are a small part of the institution's budget, some administrators resort to the practice of "leveraging" to maximize the impact of resources. For example, a certain amount of money will be provided for a piece of equipment if the amount allocated centrally will be matched by a department, a college, and even a faculty member. But this practice can have unforeseen consequences.

Faculty, departments, and colleges are not profit-making entities. It's the function of administration to prioritize the use of institutional resources and to provide the support to meet these. If fewer projects can be undertaken, then so be it. Leveraging is a means of avoiding hard decisions and is

197

Failed Grade

unfair to those departments and faculty with limited external resources.

The effective use of budgets is demanding and should not be delegated. That doesn't mean advice should not be sought. The college's budget officer and associate deans were helpful in providing a perspective for my making sounder decisions. Two heads are definitely better than one, but in the final analysis, the decision was mine. I was prepared to justify actions, not only to the faculty and staff but also to the upper administration.

Chapter Eighteen
Colleges and Universities as Money-Generating Machines

As in the corporate sector and other nonprofit organizations, academic institutions have become consumed with generating money. Such activities account for increasing amounts of time and energy of senior administrators. These institutions are becoming money-generating machines.[1] It is all part of the perceived need that money will solve all institutional problems.

Private institutions have always been involved with such activities, striving to prevent excessive increases in tuition and providing resources for scholarship funds for worthy students. Over the past twenty years, such activities have become a major commitment in public institutions also. There are several reasons: one has been the unreliability of state government in meeting its obligations, especially during sluggish economic times when tax revenues plummet. Also, they have shifted their subsidies from higher to primary and secondary education. Rather than addressing the problem facing colleges, politicians feel

Failed Grade

their reelection would be in jeopardy if taxes were increased. The percentage of the budget of public institutions provided by state government has continually declined, and university presidents perceive their public institutions becoming privatized perforce by state government.

Secondly, alumni and corporate partners perceive the importance of higher education and are willing to contribute to public as well as private institutions. Thirdly, at large public institutions, companies are interested in their research activities. They can have access to that information by contributing financially to the institution, even if the gift isn't tax-deductible. Finally, there are entertainment opportunities, especially involving big-time football and basketball programs.

Such activities in public institutions began with the creation of capital campaigns. Prior to that time, such initiatives were few, since public institutions were supported by states. However when they were successful, fundraising emerged as a major institutional activity. This is reflected in the number of personnel engaged in development activities, a fancy word for fundraising. The vice president of development at a major state university was quoted as saying,[2] "The pressure to raise funds today is relentless. Fundraising at a public university twenty years ago was an extra. It was, 'Yes, it would be nice to have it.' Now, it's becoming part of the budget."

During the period 1975-2000, university endowments increased appreciably, but with the slump in the stock market, endowments have contracted.[3] Public institutions

Colleges and Universities as Money-Generating Machines

have become dependent upon such funds for their operations. Are these resources required due to the unreliability of state support and the resources needed to curb tuition increases? Or has the institution undertaken new initiatives that require more revenue, such as building construction, centers and institutes necessitating increases in administrative, faculty, and staff personnel? Few on boards of trustees can answer those questions directly, especially as they relate to tuition increases since the budgeting process has become opaque.[4]

Development activities involve college presidents, provosts, deans, and departmental chairs as well as faculty, students, and secretarial personnel. Raising money, like any nonprofit organization, has become a major university activity, rivaling teaching and scholarship in its commitment. University presidents are selected for fundraising prowess, not their academic credentials. College deans may spend 50 percent of their time meeting and cultivating potential donors. The successful ones are prized and rewarded financially.

Faculty members recognize the importance of generating their own financial resources, not just for research and travel to professional meetings, but as a part of their salaries. In one professional college with little classroom teaching, the dean initiated what was euphemistically called "a salary-recovery plan." In effect, faculty members are expected to generate their own salary through overhead generated from grants and retained by the college. This is the ultimate in the corporate university. For a faculty member with the choice of writing another grant or

201

Failed Grade

preparing a new course for professional students, the decision is obvious. Though lip service is given to the importance of student education, faculty members have a greater impact on administrators by generating external dollars.

An instance is relevant. A friend at one institution and his colleague at another established a program researching a particular disease. They had the potential of generating significant money from federal sources. To increase that likelihood, the president at one of the universities proposed building a center, focusing specifically on that disease. The center would require a great deal of the faculty member's time, interfering with his undergraduate teaching. Though a hiring freeze prevented new faculty from being recruited, the president saw no problem. And to reduce the faculty member's teaching, he suggested the number of students in the course's other sections be increased at student expense. So much for "education."

Institutions compare themselves to one another, and public institutions are becoming competitive with their private counterparts.[3] An important measure of an institution is the size of its endowment, the money generated from alumni and friends, the extent of corporate giving, and the number of outside grants and contracts generated by faculty. All relate to money. Fundraising is an ongoing process. Colleges and universities now resemble other nonprofit organizations in that relentless activity.

Obviously, having adequate financial resources is important for any institution. However, the time devoted to that activity reflects its relative importance. Now,

Colleges and Universities as Money-Generating Machines

fundraising is more important than discussing academic goals with faculty and students. The old saying, "Actions speak louder than words" is appropriate. George Eastman, founder and CEO of Eastman Kodak, spent time walking through his plant talking with the many people, including those inserting film in a dark room. He viewed employee satisfaction as important for the company's success. In that context, one would think university presidents/provosts would be meeting regularly with faculty and students to discern the state of their institution's educational environment. Yet that no longer has the priority it once had.

Among the qualities a board of trustees listed for selecting a new president at a state university were the following: integrity, strong communication skills, smarts, a high level of energy, good judgment, and self-confidence. Without faulting the list, key attributes are missing. Not listed is the individual's record as teacher and established scholar. Does the candidate understand the need for recruiting the best faculty and know the important criteria in student education? One can't expect a public relations fundraiser to have a clear vision for where an academic institution should be heading.

When deans, department chairs, and faculty/staff are asked by senior administrators what programmatic needs are not being met, they create a wish list of personnel, scholarship funds, endowed chairs, new facilities and equipment. When these are combined from all institutional units, that becomes the basis for the institution to embark upon a major capital campaign. On the surface, this appears a rational way of identifying unmet needs. However, most

Failed Grade

academicians realize such wish lists rarely get translated into reality.

For the development officer, the wish list is a plan to present to potential donors. The objective is to tune into the interests of wealthy individuals and determine what they will support. Endowments can be tailor-made to the donor's interests since the goal is to satisfy "the customer." For the institution, unrestricted funds are preferred since their distribution becomes an administrative prerogative. Assuming a donor has provided an endowment for a particular academic unit, this would appear to indicate additional resources. That is theoretically true, but the unit's budget from the institution is not carved in stone. Frequently, part of the unit's budget is annually retrenched for various and sundry reasons.

Endowments are centrally administered. If funds are not used or their stated purpose becomes irrelevant, these are retained by administration, unless explicitly stated otherwise. Endowments can also have unexpected costs associated with them. This applies to creation of new institutes and various centers. Many, with tangential benefits to educating students, may be excellent for public relations or for corporate/university cooperation.

In one instance, an art center was created through endowment, a building was constructed, and a director hired. However, insufficient funds were available for its operation, and the institution approached the donor again to provide some of the operating costs. Institutes and centers are established and even new buildings are built, but funds required for maintenance, faculty, equipment, and their

Colleges and Universities as Money-Generating Machines

support can be inadequate and must be provided by the institution. Finally, managing these endowments becomes a challenge, especially in the current economic climate. Generating money is one issue but ensuring the maintenance of its value is another. Hiring professionals with those skills become essential for the institution.

Institutions have thus become dependent and focused on generating external funds. It is unclear the extent of need and how it is used, but senior administrators and faculty appear consumed by these activities. Proof is the amount of time spent by the president, other senior administrators, and faculty in the money chase. There is less focus on program development, where the institution should be going educationally, and whether students are being adequately prepared for a changing society. When administrators and faculty devote less time to addressing these questions than raising money, then institutional priorities are wrong and a wake-up call for colleges and universities is urgently needed.

Chapter Nineteen
The Ballooning Costs of Higher Education and Who's Worrying About It?

The cost of higher education has been rising at almost double the national inflation rate for at least a decade or more. These increases stem from the escalating costs of tuition, books, fees, room and board, and transportation, according to Ibbotson Association Inc. and the College Entrance Examination Board. Costs at private schools amount to 44 percent of the income of average middle-class families compared with 27 percent in 1980.[1] Jacques Steinberg in The New York Times on May 2, 2002, wrote in "More Family Income Committed to College" that in a study by an independent research organization, "Poor and middle-class families have had to use a steadily larger portion of their income to attend the nation's public universities over the last two decades."[2] This is echoed by

Failed Grade

Robert M. Shireman in his article,[3] "Enrolling Economic Diversity," where he says, "Today poor and middle-class families must spend nearly twice as much of their income as their counterparts did a generation ago to send their children to four-year public colleges." In fact, he reports, "poor families spent 25 percent of their annual income for their children to attend public four-year colleges in 2000 compared with 13 percent in 1980!" These comments are supported in an editorial in *The New York Times* October 23, 2002, entitled "Escalating Tuition Bills": "The public universities and colleges that grant three-quarters of this country's degrees are becoming increasingly unaffordable to the poor and working-class students who have traditionally used them to move out of poverty into the middle class. This troubling trend was underscored yet again when the College Board released alarming data showing that public-college tuition had risen by 10 percent—the largest increase in a decade."

In a letter to the editor in *The New York Times* October 27, 2002, Susan Varga, responding to *The New York Times* editorial, said, "This is leading students like me to lose faith in the mere possibility of college. They [Congress] have to realize that this is an issue that is plaguing the potential futures of thousands of students. It should be prioritized right up there with the state of the economy and the possibility of war, since it will have the same importance in the long run."

Consequently, the rate of increase in the cost of higher education is having a profound effect on access. Yet, a college education is perceived as a rite of passage for those

The Ballooning Costs of Higher Education and Who's
Worrying About It?

entering the corporate world. It is viewed as a means to a job, a career, and a financial goal. Student failures and racial, religious, and ethnic intolerance are no longer accepted. In the past, attrition of minority individuals may have stemmed from frank discrimination. The environment has changed greatly, and resources are used to recruit minorities into the student body, as well as positions into the faculty, staff, and administration. I completely support that objective; but the question is whether new administrative structures and finances expended are necessary or effective in accomplishing that goal.

A comparison of college costs for the periods 1959-60 and 1992-93 provided[4] by the U. S. Department of Education is revealing. Annette Kolodny observes,[5] "Still, even with aid, for many students, the costs of higher education are burdensome. Those from families too poor to afford the luxury of debt cannot take on even low interest education loans and are forced to work at least part time throughout their undergraduate years. And because of family necessities, too many students try to work full time while carrying a full academic course load." Both private and public colleges have had sharply rising costs that are adversely affecting the less affluent. The question is: why must the costs be so high?

Mr. James F. Carlin, former chairman of the Massachusetts Board of Higher Education, in a letter to the editor of *The New York Times* on May 12, 2002, responding to an editorial of May 5 entitled "Public Colleges, Broken Promises," said, "The reason tuition is so high is that the costs of operating our colleges and universities are

Failed Grade

ridiculously high."[6] He devotes the bulk of his letter to castigating professors, the tenure system, and shared governance and then asks administration to use 10 percent of the time devoted to fundraising "on managing their costs." The finger pointing has just begun.

Nowhere is there criticism of state boards of higher education and their failure to constrain tuition. There is plenty of blame to go around. We'll try to examine the problem in a more reasoned, substantive, and less inflammatory manner, but we must avoid being simplistic.

First, let me try to counter the assumption that the high cost of higher education is directly attributable to indolent faculty and the tenure system. Nothing could be further from the truth. I've been a tenured faculty at several institutions, an academic administrator in two universities, a scientist at a prestigious research institute and a research hospital, and a research chemist in industry and in a small startup company. Of all those positions, the hardest and most demanding was being a faculty member.

When I began teaching, I would spend ten to fifteen hours of preparation for each hour of class. Politicians without any experience in university teaching have no appreciation of what is required to do a first-class job in the classroom or laboratory. It necessitates hours in the library using books, examining original research reports, and now computer search engines to plan substantive and well-conceived courses.

Preparing good examinations that will test a student's mastery of a subject is not a simple matter. These must be graded and are especially time-consuming, when essay

210

The Ballooning Costs of Higher Education and Who's Worrying About It?

questions are involved. Then one needs to act as an advisor for students and student organizations. And of course, there is the issue of faculty scholarship, and for those in the "hard" sciences, there is the need to prepare grants for submission to national agencies since support for graduate education is directly dependent on external support. Before uninformed critics with little practical experience in college teaching begin to criticize faculty and the tenure system, they should walk in the path of the professor.

Another contributor to increased tuition costs is litigation; its impact on higher education is a recent phenomenon. In fact, most nonprofit organizations in the past were rarely sued, and legal expenses incurred did not arise from their role in a defendant capacity. In the current litigious society, that has changed, especially for colleges and universities with significant endowments. These are the attractive "deep pockets" that are an essential element in any legal suit.

In such a climate, colleges and universities have endeavored to protect themselves by hiring batteries of attorneys. Their role is not only to forestall legal suits or to mitigate their effects but also to anticipate how the institutions should respond to governmental mandates and various contractual relationships with faculty, other employees, and students. The result is additional non-teaching personnel are hired, and these costs ultimately are passed on to students via tuition increases.

Excluding the purchase of a home, the expenditure for a college education is the single most expensive item facing students and/or their parents. What key factors are

Failed Grade

contributing to the ballooning costs and who, if anyone, is doing anything about reining in these runaway expenses? That is an important issue facing higher education today.

How can the rising costs of higher education be analyzed? That is difficult from a macroeconomic perspective since there are public and private schools, small liberal arts colleges where only undergraduate education is offered, large research-oriented universities where graduate education is an important component, church-related rural schools, and large urban institutions. To mix the costs of these diverse entities and come to any meaningful conclusion is futile.

A more rational approach is to use each institution as its own control and determine changes in costs and tuition over a defined period of time. For example, one could examine the changes in the cost structure over a two-decade period. The assumption is that the mission and objectives of institutions have not materially changed. In many universities, colleges of education have schools of educational policy and leadership, one of whose focus is higher education. The ballooning higher educational costs should interest some of their faculty. They, together with those in business schools, have the requisite background to address the rising tuition costs and to probe the reasons.

Initially, one could determine whether new academic programs and institutes and centers that have been created, examine their role in student education, and determine their support from endowments. Does the institution's budget contribute to administrative, faculty, and secretarial costs for these as well as the maintenance of equipment and

*The Ballooning Costs of Higher Education and Who's
Worrying About It?*

facilities? While these new endeavors may be essential for the institution's development, if not supported by targeted income from the endowment, they add to the institution's budget contributing directly to the inflationary spiral for students.

Programs eliminated, especially with a reduction in personnel, would lower costs. Usually, these are few since initiated programs have a life of their own. Rarely are programs closed. And if any are, associated personnel frequently are transferred to other programs, keeping institutional costs essentially the same.

There are also inflationary pressures from existing programs. High-quality faculty and administrators are generally not satisfied with the status quo. They have ideas for improving programs and these involve additional costs. Their demands are understandable but must be balanced with other requirements within the institution. By determining the total costs at earlier times compared with costs at later periods provides inflation information for that program. Thus by examining all programs, one has a basis for determining the inflation rate for the institution. As already stated, education is highly labor-intensive, and generally 90 percent of the budget involves personnel. It is pertinent to examine what has occurred to personnel budgets in this time frame.

Obviously, there are costs derived from nonacademic programs, such as the creation of new centers and institutes that must be considered. There are costs originating from non-funded government mandates. In addition, there are expenditures associated with advertising and recruitment

Failed Grade

activities, office of personnel services, institutional administration and travel, development activities, legal expenses, purchasing, construction, facility maintenance, and alumni. Also, "security" has become a major priority at most colleges. The focus to this point has been on costs. The other side of the coin is income.

All income sources should be considered. These include income from tuition, overhead income from grants and contracts, income from endowment, and miscellaneous income from property and services. Knowing expenses and income should permit an understanding of why the inflation rate for higher education remains at such an elevated level even with continual fundraising. Except for scholarship funds for the few, fundraising appears to have little impact on tuition increases for all students. The apparent reason is money from these campaigns is not necessarily used to restrain tuition growth for all but may be used for new initiatives that showcase the institution's dynamism.

Attempting to probe precisely what changes have occurred and whether these are having an inflationary impact on college education, I examined the institution where I had been an academic administrator and a faculty member over a twenty-one-year period. It is representative of larger public universities. I used the archives at The Ohio State University to examine the current funds budgets of the university for the periods 1970-71, 1990-91, and for 2001-02.[7,8]

Recognizing the difficulty in comparing such time periods, since accounting processes can vary from one administration to the next,[7c] the institutional mission

*The Ballooning Costs of Higher Education and Who's
Worrying About It?*

seemingly hadn't changed. Even though new programs and institutes had been created and, more recently, "restricted" rather than "open" admission is operative, there was enough similarity between different time periods in the same institution so certain elements could be compared. The initial focus was on personnel costs since, as stated, teaching colleges in universities are highly labor-intensive.

In colleges where salary costs of faculty/staff associated with teaching are listed separately from those involved with administration, it is possible to determine the percentage of personnel costs associated with teaching and administration and their changes over the two decades from 1970 to 1990. For six of the nineteen colleges where this information was readily available for both time periods, in 1970-71, the average administrative component was 4.2 percent of the total personnel budget. By 1990-91, the average for the same units was 9.9 percent, indicating administrative personnel costs in colleges involved in teaching more than doubled over the earlier period. Clearly, a greater percentage of institutional resources are now being expended on administration.

To demonstrate how labor-intensive teaching units are, instructional personnel costs as a percentage of the total budget were determined. For the nineteen colleges from 1970 through 1971, the instructional personnel budgets, as a percentage of the total budget, ranged from 79.4 to 95.9 with an average of 90.2 percent. For the period 1990-91, the percentage of the total budget expended on personnel and their benefits in the same units ranged from 84.5 to 99.6 with an average of 92.6 percent. Though the

215

Failed Grade

differences between the two decades are small, the trend, during periods of financial contractions, is to reduce operating and equipment budgets in order to preserve teaching personnel.

There are certain non-teaching units that are directly involved in supporting the instructional mission of the institution. These include university college, academic affairs, student affairs, libraries, and graduate school. The average of the personnel budgets for these units as a percentage of their total budget was generally lower than for those involved in instruction. Comparing the total budgets of the teaching units with the teaching-support units, the latter for the 1970-71 period was 18.0 percent of the total of both. By contrast, in the period 1990-91, the percentage for the teaching-support units amounted to 21.5 percent of the total budgets for these same two decade periods. In effect, as with administration within colleges, more of the total budget is now being expended on administrative-support units than in direct support of instruction.

Finally, it is pertinent to examine increases in the personnel budgets for the teaching colleges compared with other units over this same twenty-year period since resource allocation is a good indicator of institutional priorities. Over two decades, the percentage increase in the personnel budgets for the teaching colleges ranged from 191 to 524 percent, with the average being 335 percent. During this same time span, office of the president and special events increased 449 percent; safety, security, fire, and police protection rose 540 percent; personnel in the

The Ballooning Costs of Higher Education and Who's Worrying About It?

architect's office increased 755 percent; the office of academic affairs rose over 1000 percent; and development and communication personnel increased over 1800 percent. This budgetary trend is unmistakable and is summarized in the table below.

Summary of Average Percentage Increase in Personnel Costs 1970-71 to 1990-91

Teaching Colleges	335
Office of the President and Special Events	449
Safety, Security, Fire, and Police	540
Architect's Office	755
Academic Affairs	1000
Development and Communications	1800

It is not my desire to make value judgments regarding these budgetary allocations, but these are the facts. What is apparent is financial support of teaching as a percentage of the institution's total budget has declined from 1970-71 to 1990-91. Moreover, some administrative units, especially development activities, have been greatly expanded.

Failed Grade

Unfortunately, it was not possible to do such an analysis from the data presented for 2001-02.[7c]

One rationale proposed for the massive increase in development activities is that state government has been progressively reducing support of higher education, especially during times of economic contraction. This has been painfully apparent during the recessions of 2001 and 2002. Yet, the resources generated from development activities have apparently not been used to increase compensation of existing faculty or to reduce the increase in tuition for all students.

Who, then, is doing something about the ballooning tuition costs and rising student debt during and after college? With rare exception, little is being done at most institutions. Let's examine the players.

Are faculty members concerned about tuition inflation? Do they offer to teach more courses so fewer faculty members are needed? They do not, because they are not evaluated or rewarded by that criterion. Though there are teaching awards and lip service is given to the importance of teaching, a faculty member's value in many major institutions is based upon scholarship and the number of grants and contracts obtained.

Teaching is viewed as a necessary distraction, not the priority it should be, regardless of what administrators say. The important yardstick in faculty evaluation is obtained by examining salary increments and to whom the largest increases are given. This tells an individual's importance to the institution. Those generating more grants and contracts get larger salary increases than those with heavier teaching

*The Ballooning Costs of Higher Education and Who's
Worrying About It?*

responsibilities. The message is clear regarding the institution's priority. So, if the choice for a faculty member is developing a new course for which there is a need or writing a grant proposal, the decision is obvious.

Are college administrators concerned about tuition increases and what are they doing to dampen administrative increases? Do they reduce the number of staff personnel or curb their university-funded travel? That hasn't occurred. On the contrary, the size of the administrative budget is increasing at a much greater rate than any other component. An interesting example is shown for the public universities of Illinois[9] where the size of administration increased ten times the rate for teaching positions in the decade between fiscal years 1993 and 2003.

Administrators create new centers and institutes requiring the recruitment of senior and high-salaried personnel. These entities generally have no impact on undergraduate education and little, if any, on graduate and professional education. They enhance the institution's reputation, help in fundraising activities, and may be done for public relations reasons. They usually serve little educational purpose but certainly add to institutional costs.

The same applies to the construction of most new buildings. There is a confluence of interests in state-funded institutions between politicians and the construction industry, which strongly favor such activities. Likewise at private institutions, wealthy alumni donate money for new construction with the stipulation that their names appear on the buildings. Administrators and faculty want modern facilities, but maintaining these requires additional

Failed Grade

continuing budget support that is not forthcoming from endowment or state agencies.

Institutions, with the exception of the small number of students receiving scholarships, have done little in dampening tuition increases. The academic plan proposed in The Ohio State University budget for 2001-02 cites[10] "resident undergraduate tuition and fees at Ohio State are 3.8% below the benchmark average in FY 2001" (where nine benchmark public institutions are used for comparison) and "are 5.4% below the state average. This makes Ohio State an excellent value for students and taxpayers but it also means Ohio State does not have the resources to match our competition in key academic and support areas." On this basis, tuition was increased 9.3 percent in FY 2002, 15.4 percent in FY 2003,[11] and 13.4 percent in FY 2004 for in-state students.[12] This amounts to a tuition increase of over 38 percent for this three- year period.

In general, tuition is based on institutional expenses, and if the choice is between creating additional centers and institutes, recruiting "star" senior research faculty and new institutional initiatives, or limiting tuition charges for the many, the former always wins out. Of course universities should be innovative and at the cutting-edge of new developments. But not all new initiatives can be funded. They must be prioritized to ensure that tuition remains affordable to the bright and less affluent students.

Boards of trustees, the final arbiters on budgets, have little appreciation for establishing institutional priorities. They have minimal understanding of personnel

The Ballooning Costs of Higher Education and Who's Worrying About It?

requirements of the institution or the need for administrative travel. So, tuition increases are generally whatever the institutional administrators recommend to the board. Tuition is analogous to cost plus contracts. The institution determines its needs and passes on the charges to the students. Since most institutions function similarly, one can't expect differential treatment between public or private institutions or competition among institutions with respect to tuition. Thus, financial pressures for students are unfortunately not of great concern to faculty, administrators, or members of the boards of trustees. The board's lack of action demonstrates the relative unimportance of tuition increases.

In public institutions, where tuition is subsidized by public expenditures, politicians have little concern for rising tuition costs. The central purpose of land-grant institutions, where college education was conceived for all, regardless of ability to pay, is being gutted by inaction of elected officials. Politicians when faced with the choice of increasing taxes to maintain tuition or passing tuition increases on to students, the latter always predominates. Students have a lower priority than a lawmaker's reelection.

Savings in the higher-education budget might also be achieved if the state boards of higher education consolidated the number of institutions and programs receiving state support. However, once institutions are state supported, they remain so in perpetuity. Raising tuition is less painful than the political fallout from eliminating state support for any institution, regardless of its quality. So,

Failed Grade

state boards of higher education or boards of regents take the path of least resistance, allowing tuition to rise in preference to any other alternative.

Does the electorate care about tuition costs? Only students and their parents who are impacted are concerned, but after graduation, they show little concern. Others feel it is not their problem. In reality, there is insufficient concern in any constituency to cause this matter to have a high priority, and so little has been done. Many students now graduate from colleges and universities, especially the less affluent, with significant debt and work for years to pay it off. Some people never get a college education even if qualified. We've placed on the backs of young people problems that should be dealt with by society.

Like many issues, we only address them in times of crisis. That time is fast approaching for college costs. It will occur when college education becomes accessible to fewer people, despite society's need for a highly educated workforce. Only then will the matter of access appear on the radar screen. This problem should be addressed now with all constituencies: faculty, administrators, trustees, members of the board of regents, and politicians, sitting together, accepting that each has a vital interest in solving this problem. Budgets and the budgeting process must be totally transparent and not opaque, as they have become. The parties must collaborate now to reduce or at least restrict the growth of institutional costs to minimize the exploding cost of a college education.

Chapter Twenty
The Legacy of Faculty and Academic Administrators

The legacy of those associated with colleges and universities is clear. As Allan Bloom(Reference 1 below) has said, "There is no need to prove the importance of education; but it should be remarked that for modern nations, which have founded themselves on reason in its various uses more than did any nations in the past, a crisis in the university, the home of reason, is perhaps the profoundest crisis they face."[1] The value of higher education to society need not be debated; but how do various participants view their contributions in retrospect?

Legacy of Faculty
As a faculty member, one's legacy is different than departing administrators. The best faculty members are remembered by students for their concern in providing excellent education and by high academic standards. The

Failed Grade

better ones genuinely care about students and are sensitive to their needs as for their own children.

I knew one faculty member who was greatly beloved. He and his wife had welcomed graduate and undergraduate students into their home. He established high standards in his courses, carefully monitoring student performance. He gave unstintingly to students, helping them master new concepts and always available to them. He was concerned not only with their academic performance but their personal lives. Foreign students especially felt a singular bond to him.

When he retired, former students from everywhere came to that retirement dinner. Their affection and love was palpable. One successful former undergraduate established an endowed chair in his name; others gave support for a graduate fellowship recognizing his scholarly accomplishments. Even after his death, former students regularly sought out his widow. He cared about these students and gave them an appreciation of the importance of lifelong learning. He had made a difference in their lives. The students are one of the legacies of a faculty member.

A second legacy can be the quality of scholarship. Is that scholarship recognized and appreciated by one's peers and others in the society? This can be demonstrated in the form of publications, presentations, patents awarded, and, of course, various honors and other recognitions. One's scholarly legacy can be the tangible accomplishments produced over decades.

This scholarship has been created by hard work and will be enduring long after the faculty member has departed.

The Legacy of Faculty and Academic Administors

There are also the clinical/educators who may have a beneficial effect on their patients as well as their students and are fondly remembered for what they did. What is the legacy of the academic administrator?

Administrative Legacy

The administrator is frequently remembered more for failures than successes. Failures arise from a lack of perception, the intrusion of political considerations in one's decisions, ethical lapses, or sheer laziness. Appointment of deans and department chairs that are politically motivated can be destructive and will be remembered. There is never an urgent need to appoint any administrator, especially when gnawing questions remain regarding his/her administrative potential.

My wife says the expression "good enough" is an oxymoron. Why should one accept "good enough" when better people are available? One is reminded of the old saw relating to quick marriages: "Select in haste; repent at leisure."

It is usually preferable to appoint acting administrators from within an organization than selecting outside individuals, without confidence they will perform admirably. Insecure institutions think outside people are preferable to those from within. I asked one provost, departing to become president at another institution, why many institutions felt compelled to go outside an institution to recruit senior administrators. He said they were insecure and held a low opinion of those within. Familiarity breeds contempt.

225

Failed Grade

I knew administrators who when supervising departments and colleges, terminated incompetent administrators even if they had been the ones who had appointed them. In other words, they were not wedded to their own appointees but based decisions on the individual's performance. In one case, a dean's resignation was requested eighteen months after his appointment by the provost who had appointed him.

Such administrators had high standards and a well-deserved positive legacy. Since administrators serve only with the concurrence and support of those above them, these positions have no tenure, nor should they. Retaining failed deans and department chairs indicates incompetence, laziness, or both by provosts and presidents.

Sometimes there may be a lack of courage due to litigious concerns or an unwillingness to confront unpleasant terminations. The result is the same and vital decisions are either avoided altogether or postponed. One would expect at the time of possible reappointment, individuals who have performed ineffectively could be told they will not be continuing.

That permits a face-saving resignation. I have witnessed weak presidents or provosts at one institution either reappointed with a significant salary increase or appointed at even more prestigious institutions. Inertia is a common failing at academic institutions.

Awarding weak faculty permanent positions and errors made in tenure decisions result in adversely affecting the learning environment and collegiality of the organization. Mediocre faculty members have little mobility and can stay

The Legacy of Faculty and Academic Administors

in departments for their entire academic career. Their presence is not conducive to attracting and retaining good students or new superior faculty. When excellent potential faculty members perceive a collection of faculty who, in effect, are retired, why would they be attracted to that unit? Such individuals are euphemistically called "dead wood;" more appropriately, they are petrifying.

Obviously, no administrator purposefully retains nonproductive, untenured faculty. Signs of ossification are observed early. If in doubt, err on the side of future students, successors, and colleagues and encourage marginal faculty members to leave the institution early. Similarly, there is no reason to retain unproductive staff. Why would any administrator keep ineffective people? One reason perhaps is these employees are non-threatening to the marginal administrator—they never challenge the boss.

I knew one administrator who worked diligently to create a high-quality environment. By many criteria he was judged to be successful. But his successor discouraged new ideas from faculty and staff, focusing on his own perquisites. Travel funds previously used to send faculty and staff to professional meetings were now used for administrative travel. Collaboration and cooperation within the unit was no longer seen as being valuable. The better faculty and staff looked to other institutions.

This administrator's predecessor complained to his friends as to what had happened to his former unit. He should have realized the truth of Lord Krishna's dictum, "It is your right to do your duty but not to expect the fruits of your labor."[2] Though imitation is the most sincere form of

Failed Grade

flattery, the expectation that future administrations will be modeled after a previously successful one can be unrealistic.

In contrast with those of faculty, the legacy of administrators is transient. One university president spent four hours after each graduation having his picture taken with every graduate and their families. He wished to ensure his own legacy.

Good administrators would like to be remembered for their accomplishments, not unlike good teachers. However, even for successful ones, their administrations are like sand castles on the beach of time ready to be eroded or disappear altogether by the tidal wave of the new, incoming administration. There is no administrative permanence. Maybe it is for this reason that compensation, perquisites, and retirement benefits have become the important yardsticks by which administrators measure their success.

Chapter Twenty-One
The Murky Future of Higher Education in the United States

Any attempt to predict the future for any institution, let alone higher education, is at best tenuous. No one is sufficiently clairvoyant to know what the environment will be in 2020 except by 20/20 hindsight. However, current trends may give indications as to the future environment.[1] The more significant of these has been the corporatization of our colleges and universities, a consuming focus on money generation, and the perceived need to be on the "right" side of every social and political issue. The consequences are that marketing and public relations matters have greater prominence than educational values. This chapter will necessarily be somewhat repetitive because it is a summary, but at the same time, there are suggested changes for the improvement of higher education. Among the activities that are highlighted are

Failed Grade

athletics, students, faculty, administration, and the organization.

Athletics

Intercollegiate athletics play a minor role or none at all at the University of Chicago, Massachusetts Institute of Technology, Johns Hopkins University, California Institute of Technology, the University of Rochester, and at some Ivy League institutions. Yet a number of students are attracted to them because they can combine a high quality education with athletic competition.

On the other hand, big-time football and basketball programs have only minimal objectives in common with academic programs. The former are only about entertainment. When teams lose their competitive edge and no longer entertain, coaches are terminated, regardless of the given reasons.

Some recent books have recounted the problems facing universities with big-time athletic programs: Intercollegiate Athletics and the American University. A University President's Perspective[2] by James J. Duderstadt, The Game of Life: College Sports and Educational Values[3] by James L. Shulman and William G. Bowen, and Beer and Circus: How Big-Time College Sports Is Crippling Undergraduate Education[4] by Murray Sperber.

Compensation of coaches and their staffs is far greater than that of other faculty. Coaches can be as comfortable working for owners of professional sport teams, with no academic purpose, as they are in colleges and universities since their salaries are comparable. Faculty members have

The Murky Future of Higher Education in the United States

no responsibility in controlling these programs, and it is doubtful whether university presidents do as well.[5]

Interestingly enough, athletic programs are the only place in higher education where superior performance and elitism are unabashedly trumpeted. Excellence is the sole requirement, and coaches can dismiss people from the team if there is a lack of ability or effort or when academic programs interfere with their commitment to athletics. In academic matters, elitism still must be defended.[6]

How long colleges and universities will remain in big-time athletics depends on pressure from the public and the attitudes of university presidents, alumni, and politicians. But their relationship to the educational mission is tangential. A column by Albert R. Hunt in the February 1, 2001, issue of *The Wall Street Journal* quoted the director of admissions at Williams College that athletic recruitment was "the biggest form of Affirmative Action in higher education." If true, that is scandalous.

Most young male students recruited into football and basketball programs are not wealthy and need scholarships to come to college. For basic living expenses, they can become prey to unscrupulous agents and unethical alumni since student athletes are too busy conditioning themselves and practicing to have a useful part-time job. Those abuses have already been seen. The charade that they are amateurs and not professionals is just that and a more reasonable solution must be found. For their services, student athletes should be paid. And if not, why not?

They possess financial value to the institution and are not there simply to get an education. Just as graduate

Failed Grade

students are given a stipend as graduate assistants to assist professors in educating undergraduates, grading examinations, and in carrying out laboratory research, so too student athletes should be recruited as athletic assistants and given a four-year assistantship.

Since many won't have time to devote fully to academics and obtain a degree, a four-year academic scholarship should be awarded upon the completion of the entire assistantship. Students leaving their assistantship before four years will forfeit the scholarship provision.

The number of athletic assistantships and the amount of the stipend awarded must be established and controlled by the NCAA or some other oversight committee to ensure all students and schools are treated fairly. Since most student athletes never reach the professional level, the scholarship provision would give them the opportunity to obtain a college degree in a program based upon their academic interests. This issue should be addressed honestly, and directly now. It is unethical for the institutions to continue to exploit largely minority and poor young men with little concern for their professional future. And if not now, when?

Another matter relates to the involvement of women in intercollegiate athletics.[7] Title IX of the Higher Education Act established the justification for gender equity in women's varsity athletics. Elimination of athletic programs for men to achieve gender parity has been an unfortunate consequence. Yet, it is unfair to penalize those men with an interest in minor sports. This legacy of the intrusion of a prescriptive legal system where one size fits all discounts

The Murky Future of Higher Education in the United States

variations among colleges and experimentation by faculty and administrators in determining what is right for each institution. Fear of litigation is driving the process.

Finally, uncontrolled growth in spending, especially on football and basketball programs, contributes to the athletic tail wagging the academic dog. This development is undesirable and unsustainable. It is time that there be a cap upon all athletic budgets and further increases should be strictly inflation based.

Students
To adapt Charles Dickens's, *A Tale of Two Cities*, "It *is* the best of times, it *is* the worst of times, it *is* the age of wisdom, it *is* the age of foolishness—." Such is the current environment college students are experiencing.

1. Diversity
The prejudices and discriminations of the past have disappeared or are rapidly disappearing. Colleges and universities are clearly one of the more diverse, tolerant, and least biased of any institution in society today. Yet legacies of distrust are not easily erased from the consciousness of those affected.

Affirmative action programs designed to correct past injustices have been implemented with varying degrees of success, and further experimentation by colleges and universities is needed to arrive at a fair admission's policy. Institutions want a diverse student body but they are meeting legal challenges by those denied access. Ideally, the institutions and not the courts should determine the

Failed Grade

most appropriate way of dealing with past discriminations. Previously discriminated women are now found in every college and discipline and are the most successful segment to overcome discrimination.

The situation for minorities is not so advanced. Many disciplines have few African-American, Hispanic, and Native Americans, especially in the physical sciences, engineering, and health professions. Their numbers do not provide a sufficient pool for graduate and professional studies, thereby limiting their availability for faculty positions. A better job must be done sensitizing students in earlier grades to the professional opportunities available. Many have sufficient native ability but need a more supportive learning environment. A more effective job must be done to counter destructive peer pressure equating learning with rejection of one's culture.

One important point: diversity must not occur at the expense of quality. There are bright and competent individuals from every racial, religious, and ethnic grouping. Merit must be at the heart of the academic enterprise. Compromising quality to achieve diversity would do a disservice to all and especially to the long-term environment in colleges and universities. Students will rise to meet the standards expected of them, provided these are enunciated at the outset and administered fairly.

Academic institutions should support not only the diversity of people but also the diversity of ideas. Colleges and universities must be places where issues and ideas are critically debated but also where there is respect and tolerance for different views. Such an environment prepares

234

The Murky Future of Higher Education in the United States

future graduates to think for themselves and to function in a diverse and pluralistic world. Diversity should be viewed as a means to an educational end and not an end itself. Institutions must discourage politicization or balkanization of the student body on campus. Useful educational experiences cannot be achieved in isolation. The function of colleges must be to promote integration as enunciated by Dr. Martin Luther King, Jr., in his "I Have a Dream Speech." Administrative leadership is required if all students are to be prepared for a multicultural society.

2. Access

A major problem facing higher education today is the cost of college. The inflation rate has far exceeded other expenditures over decades. As Robert and Jon Solomon stated,[8] "University tuition has gone up twice the rate of inflation over the past decade" and faster more recently.

State support has plummeted[9] with the states' contribution to budgets for universities in Michigan, Virginia, and Wisconsin, ranging from 10 to 25 percent. Money already allocated is not secure, for example Oklahoma University.[10] Administration can either raise tuition (University of Iowa increased tuition 18 percent) or reduce faculty/staff. Sometimes both are being done.[11] Miami University in Ohio doubled in-state tuition. With shrinking state support, tuition is skyrocketing.[12] The concept of the land-grant institution is disappearing. David Leonhardt noted,[13] "More members of this year's freshman class at the University of Michigan have parents making at least $200,000 a year than have parents making less than

235

Failed Grade

the national median of about $53,000." Prepaid tuition plans, when available, are being impacted as rates have risen by 7 percent.[14]

Although there are scholarship funds, many students grapple with providing their own resources for education. Part-time and even full-time jobs become necessary, in addition to loans. Escalating costs make less expensive distance learning an option,[15] even though these have their own limitations.

The continual rise in tuition has not been seriously addressed by all constituencies, including state legislatures and governors. Politicians create new institutions in districts benefiting them politically but also generating additional costs for the higher education budget. When it is necessary to ensure affordable tuition, politicians become profiles in cowardice, hiding behind the mantra of "no new taxes."

State boards of higher education, which should have responsibility for creating new institutions, are never asked, "Are there too many state-supported institutions already based on the available budget?" "Are there too many undergraduate, professional, and graduate programs and can some be coalesced, benefiting program quality and cost?"[16] The public has a right to know whether the higher-education budget in a state is prudently used and why tuition costs are out-of-control.

It is clear the issue of student access is one of major importance and must be addressed by all constituencies involved in higher education. Increased pressure on young people to go to college and pay for their education has

The Murky Future of Higher Education in the United States

resulted in college becoming a part-time activity. Leadership is required if this problem is to be dealt with effectively and timely.

3. Career Options

An increasing number of career options are available to students. How can the options be sorted out so students are prepared to make rational decisions? It is a dilemma facing many students today.

Enjoying and doing well in certain courses is only one part of the equation. Can one extrapolate to determining whether one will enjoy and be successful in a particular career? That is the critical question. My advice is that students follow their strengths and interests in selecting potential careers. Even so, it is difficult to know just from didactic courses if the career chosen will be the right one. Cooperative education is one possibility, since there is no substitute for practical work experiences. Many college students rarely experience the practical side of a career before making a choice. I remember saying flippantly after completing my doctorate, "I will only go into teaching if I have no new research ideas." It was a comment based on ignorance since I spent more than thirty years in education and enjoyed it very much. Even so, professions and their environments are continually changing and these changes can have important effects on job satisfaction.

Is there a solution to this conundrum? Probably there is no one answer for every person. One recommendation is to obtain a broad education in college including practical experiences. These will be growth promoting and may be

Failed Grade

useful in sorting through the expanding career maze. At the same time, one shouldn't become an educational dilettante. Real decisions must be made regarding choices. It is not the worst decision to select a career, but be prepared for a different career pathway after a reasonable time.

Colleges have been woefully inadequate in providing sound career counseling. Faculty, administration, and alumni could be enormously helpful, yet are rarely used by students. I recently met a student serving as a part-time waiter in a restaurant. I inquired about his career interests and on learning of them, I asked whether he had talked with an internationally renowned faculty member in his college with expertise in that area. He didn't know him but promised to contact him for advice with his program.

4. Student Attitudes and Expectations

For students a college education is considered a means to a well-paying job. Unfortunately, this short-sighted approach results in students wanting minimal challenges. College should be a time for maximizing one's education since one never knows when the education will be useful. The objective should be to gain as much as one can from the experience.

Students increasingly view themselves as consumers. In *The University in a Corporate Culture*, Eric Gould discusses[17] the impact that corporate culture and student consumerism are having on higher education. A degree is viewed as "a market-driven commodity" and no longer an educational process. In that context, it is understandable that students want to be treated with the rights and

The Murky Future of Higher Education in the United States

privileges accorded to "customers." Such attitudes have influenced grading even at prestigious schools. Harvard's president, Lawrence Summers, cited the need for strengthening and improving undergraduate education by stiffening the grading system.[18] Now, there can almost be a compact between students, administration, and some faculty that C grades are the lowest one should receive. For many students as well, they take longer than four years to obtain a degree especially as college becomes a part-time activity.

These are some of the factors impacting students and in turn, institutions. Foremost is the institution's role as gatekeeper, ensuring only those qualified graduate. Anything less does a disservice to the students, the organization that recruits them, and the entire society. Preparing the next generation for careers and the environment after college is no easy task, but maintaining high standards is the responsibility of colleges and universities.

Faculty
1. Compensation and Diversity

For faculty this is also the best of times and the worst of times. Salaries have never been higher despite the fact that many older faculty are not keeping pace with inflation. Still, the need to attract and retain superior people with a strong interest in academia remains. Recruitment of faculty, staff, and administrators is governed by a desire to include all segments of society. Women are found in every

Failed Grade

discipline and level as faculty members and in upper administration.

This hopeful sign shows the battle may soon be won and the need to address women's issues and discrimination in universities may soon be a thing of the past. However, objective criteria are needed to determine when that time has arrived. Only then will it be appropriate to question whether administrative structures and time devoted to gender equality issues are still relevant.

Recruitment of Black and Hispanic faculty, especially in the sciences, engineering, and health professions, is completely different. The pool from which faculty are drawn is totally inadequate. Recruiting from one institution to another of the small pool available is analogous to a game of musical chairs without any benefit to the academic enterprise and its goal of population diversity.

2. Governance, Tenure and Unionization

With respect to governance and tenure, this is not the best of times. Shared governance between administration and faculty is gradually being eroded as the corporate structure is becoming firmly established. Faculty governance is viewed as an impediment to decision making by presidents, provosts, and deans with more decisions made unilaterally by administrators.

The argument is made that institutions must be "nimble." Yet universities are not vying with commercial enterprises where rapid decisions must be made or success will be compromised. When faculty members are opposed to an administrator's position, the matter is raised

The Murky Future of Higher Education in the United States

repeatedly until the result desired by the administrator is approved. That process is not shared governance but administrative manipulation.

The complaint that involving faculty in decisions is too cumbersome is a canard. Faculty members are accustomed to preparing courses and examinations on time and to meeting deadlines for grant proposals. Administrators can impose timelines for important decisions by the faculty; discussion and debate doesn't have to be open-ended. The reason for not involving faculty is the administrators' fear of their rejection of new administrative initiatives. It is easier not to involve faculty than to overrule their cogent objections.

The result is more faculty members withdraw from the governance process. In the past, faculty committees were central to all academic decisions. Now, many faculty members see little value in attending faculty meetings, which are perceived as sham governance. As a result, faculty members have decreased interest in institutional needs and no longer feel part of "the family." One symptom of faculty alienation is that many have opted for early retirement. Such programs exacerbate the loss of institutional memory resulting in junior faculty no longer being acculturated by their senior colleagues.

Tenure is also under increasing attack, being viewed as a serious impediment to cost control. Increasing numbers of individuals are classified as "clinical" faculty, even if not in health-related disciplines. Such faculty may not be subjected to peer review in recruitment and thus can be terminated more easily.

Failed Grade

It is apparent that there is growing dissatisfaction by many faculty members with the corporate environment. Not only is there loss in faculty governance and a major focus on money generation, but also traditional faculty control of academic standards is under pressure. This may presage a greater move toward unionization. Whereas, faculty unionization has been the exception rather than the rule in higher education, a major shift of power from faculty to administrators and increased tension could fuel such a movement. Unionization is the strongest indicator of administrative incompetence.

Such a trend would have serious long-term consequences for the learning environment. Those colleges and universities already unionized have an adversarial relationship between faculty and administration, an environment where everything must be formally negotiated. Normally, most individuals do not choose to place an intermediary between themselves and administrators, unless they feel powerless to influence events and have concluded this is the only way to have their voice heard.

To reverse these directions, I suggest that the chief academic officer, the senior vice president for academic affairs or provost, be elected directly by the faculty instead of being selected by the president. This position should be for a five-year period with the option for no more than a single second term. Implicit in this proposal is that the provost or vice president for academic affairs would be a senior faculty member or administrator from within the

The Murky Future of Higher Education in the United States

college or university and not some outside individual with little understanding of the institution.

Just as selection would be made by the faculty, removal could also occur by a similar process. It would ensure that faculty members have a major stake in university governance, and under such conditions, education of students may again regain its primacy. That does not mean scholarly and research activities should be denigrated. Far from it, but the purpose of grants and contracts would be for the education of students and not merely because of the overhead generated.

Administration
1. Compensation and Environment
With respect to administrative compensation, this is the best of times. Salaries have never been higher, as are differentials between administrators and faculty. The downside for those ultimately wanting to return to faculty ranks is they would be disadvantaged financially. As a consequence, movement from faculty to administration has become a one-way street. The easy interaction between faculty and administrators of the past has been altered. Administrators now are more focused on their role as entrepreneurs and financial managers. Academic units are viewed as "profit centers." Each program is required to sit "on its own bottom" and program justification is based largely on financial solvency.

An administrator's prowess in fundraising has become the important yardstick for recruitment and measuring administrative success. Consequently, department

Failed Grade

administrators, particularly in the sciences, are more interested in patenting faculty research than having results published early. This is a disadvantage to graduate students and postdoctoral fellows who must wait for their work to be published. Patents, if commercialized, offer financial reward to the researcher, the department, and the institution.[19]

Rampant commercialization did not occur by happenstance. It is, I think, the product of inept leadership where university administrators have become addicted especially to overhead money from grants and contracts. Financial imperatives have become exacerbated as major corporations with no long-term commitment invest in premier academic institutions. Their reason is potential profit. Resources provided are attractive, even if they are one-time only, since the institution has the possibility of sharing in future commercialization.[20]

In such a climate, educating students appears of secondary importance. Students who contribute to the institution's research productivity are prized. Their education becomes a byproduct of research, not an end in itself. Obviously, this is a sharply drawn scenario, but many institutions are moving in that direction.

Since the board of trustees has ultimate responsibility for the institution's environment, they must continually monitor the effectiveness of the president. They cannot do that in isolation but must identify the key constituencies among the faculty and determine their perception of the institution's environment. There must be strict confidentiality of such sensitive discussions if the faculty's

The Murky Future of Higher Education in the United States

views are to be honest and forthright. Although termination of a president may be disruptive, it is preferable to the retention of someone who is incompetent.

2. Technology

The full influence of technology on teaching in colleges and universities is barely on the horizon. The effects of distance learning, the Internet, and chat rooms together with broadband communication present new opportunities and challenges for the administrators and institutions. In the past, universities decentralized and offered a variety of courses on branch campuses. However, most upper-level courses and especially graduate courses were available only at the central campus. Students matriculating at branch campuses transferred to the central campus for such offerings.

With the development of fiber-optic, video, and wireless communication and the potential for video conferencing, it is possible for one professor to communicate with students anywhere. The most effective teachers in the future may become independent contractors, offering to lecture and interact with students at any locality and institution. Colleges, universities, and even for-profit corporations may contract with such "star" educators offering courses for credit that ultimately may lead to a degree. What kind of administrative oversight can institutions, let alone state boards of higher education, provide when programs can originate from locations out of state and even out of the country? This will be an important question for college

Failed Grade

administrators when distance learning courses become well established.

As higher education becomes more expensive and more mature people with time and location constraints want an education, distance learning becomes an attractive alternative. Its effect on certain programs could be profound and must be considered by administrators. Technology influenced how banking changed to meet societal needs. That can apply also to didactic instruction in colleges. The methods for delivering education will not remain static, and institutions will need to adapt to this new reality.

Technology also applies to research equipment, necessary in educating students for high technology positions. Although administrative structures are approaching the corporate model, the planning, purchasing, maintenance, access, and amortization of research equipment are still in the horse-and-buggy era in academic settings, compared with how such equipment is acquired and maintained in industry. One main reason is that academic administrators authorizing equipment purchases generally don't have a background in the physical and biological sciences, or if they do, their prior experience is no longer relevant.

Research equipment at academic institutions is frequently costly and generally acquired on a one-time-only basis. The prime mover for its acquisition may be a person having grant money, thus controlling both location and availability. Others can experience difficulty in gaining access since there is little administrative coordination,

The Murky Future of Higher Education in the United States

despite the fact that the equipment was purchased by the institution.

The result is an inefficient and costly system with little administrative oversight. Equipment needed may be postponed or, when acquired, purchased multiple times to ensure access by students and faculty. At one time, when I was trying to provide electron microscopic services for some faculty, we learned there were ten to twelve electron microscopes in the health science complex. However, only two were in operating condition, and these were unavailable except to the individual in charge of the equipment.

If academic institutions are to be at the cutting-edge of knowledge, a more efficient system must be instituted. It is my suggestion that a vice president for research or some knowledgeable individual have ultimate responsibility for acquisition, location, maintenance, amortization, and access of all major research equipment. Such a person could ensure that there was no unnecessary duplication and that purchase of expensive capital equipment would be carefully planned.

3. Austerity and Budgetary Contractions
Probably one of the best tests for administrators is how they deal with austerity and budgetary contractions. At state institutions, these are inevitable with changing economic conditions. The priorities administrators set are indicative of what they think is important. When serving on a search committee for a senior administrator in the university, I asked an applicant how he would prioritize

Failed Grade

budgetary reductions when they occurred. He was nonplussed by my query. Obviously, he hadn't considered such a question would ever be asked.

Greater budgetary transparency should occur, especially during times of economic contractions. Unfortunately, the budgetary process at many institutions has become increasingly opaque, shielding administrators from criticism. One can determine administrative priorities by funding and not rhetoric. And in that context, "actions speak louder than words."

If budgets must be reduced, do administrators insist on retrenching academic enrichment programs while new nonacademic centers are created? Are journals, books and libraries essential for student education and faculty scholarship reduced but administrative travel is maintained? And are faculty and staff salary increases eliminated or severely reduced and academic positions frozen while new center administrators with their staffs are being hired?

The administrator gives a clear signal what is important. In my view, the first place to cut is within one's own administrative structure. The objective is to preserve the core academic activities and limit tuition increases. For this reason, administrative travel, additional staff, and new administrative initiatives should be postponed if not curtailed. Administrators set the example for everyone in their units.

Unfortunately, I have observed that administrative needs and interests are not affected during periods of austerity. It is for this reason that I recommend complete budget

The Murky Future of Higher Education in the United States

transparency. The vice president for finance should be prepared annually to appear before the university community and present the institution's budget. The financial support of various units and the reasons for tuition increases should be made clear to everyone. And the vice president should be prepared to answer questions from the participants.

4. Leadership

Any scenario for the future success of higher education depends upon the quality of academic leadership. Leadership is the key to environment creation. What types of people are applying for presidents of universities? What skills do they possess and what is their focus?

The Clark Kerrs of the University of California, the Robert Hutchinses of the University of Chicago, and the James Conants of Harvard University—presidents and academic giants of a bygone era—are nowhere to be found today. They probably wouldn't survive the first cut now in any presidential search. For president, boards of trustees, who are generally from the corporate world, want someone who is a public relations master, a glad-hander, an excellent communicator, ahead of politically correct curves, and above all, a supreme fundraiser. Low on the totem pole are the individual's academic accomplishments, teaching and scholarship, commitment to high standards for students, maintaining the institution's primary role in educating the next generation, and vision of the future of higher education.

Failed Grade

Search committees are often unwieldy due to past discrimination and the desire for every constituency to have a voice in the selection process of a university president. Committees can contain fifteen to twenty members or more. Such large search committees are unworkable since arranging meeting times becomes an impossible task. The consequence is institutions must rely solely on outside search firms, with mixed results.

It is my recommendation that presidential search committees be limited to six to seven members, drawn from the faculty and the board of trustees. The committee should not delegate their responsibility to those outside the institution but take an active role in identifying appropriate candidates. Because of the need to experience operationally the role of higher education in teaching, research, and service, university presidents should be drawn primarily from the academic ranks. While there are no guarantees that successful teachers and scholars will become effective administrators and presidents, the choice should be among these. Populating senior administrative positions with professional administrators, assures institutions will be led by individuals with little understanding of the intricacies of higher education and bereft of an academic vision for the future.

Organization
1. Programs
The American people have been among the most generous in the world. Higher education has been a key beneficiary. And while many organizations in the for-profit

The Murky Future of Higher Education in the United States

sector deal with severe contractions and bankruptcies, most academic institutions have not experienced such trauma. As a consequence, colleges and universities are more familiar with creating new programs than with program contraction or elimination. In the 1960s and 1970s, colleges and universities greatly proliferated. There was a "candy store" mentality then. Administrators felt driven by the need to add programs they didn't have. But it is quite a different matter when resources are reduced, requiring contraction. How is this to be accomplished? Across-the-board reduction of all programs is a prescription for mediocrity. An ongoing review initiated by administrators is essential, involving faculty, students, and even outside experts with no conflict of interest. Such a process will prevent inertia and may end programs that have outlived their usefulness. This is never a pleasant task. However, resources saved are better spent in bolstering strong programs.

Ending any program must be done in a manner sensitive to students, faculty, staff, and alumni. To terminate a program abruptly and in an unethical way reflects poorly on the administrators and the organization, damaging their public perception. For this reason, there must be collaboration with boards of higher education. Ethical, not just financial, concerns must be paramount.

2. Institutional Collaboration

Boards of regents were initially created to lessen political interference into higher education. Ironically, politicians have succeeded in doing just the opposite since board members are selected for political and not academic

Failed Grade

attributes. Yet boards can and should play a major role in assisting institutions in the maintenance of quality and in fostering inter-institutional collaboration.

When institutions decide to terminate a program, it would be important to gain assistance from a state board of higher education. Eliminating a program at one institution while supporting a higher quality one at another can be beneficial to the entire system. Since people in that program would be adversely affected there must be a sufficient time horizon in the transition. As a first step, no new students or faculty should be recruited into that program. Students already in the program must be permitted to complete it. It is my view that faculty should be given the option of transferring from the program being closed to the institution where it is offered. Those permanent faculty who do not wish to transfer, may be granted tenure in another department in their present institution. Faculty members who must be terminated from their present institution must be given special consideration. Cooperation and less competition among institutions would facilitate such program transfers.

The basic concept is institutions should not view themselves as completely separate entities but part of the higher-educational establishment in the state. Institutional collaboration has not been significant in the past. But with limited resources, it is critical that institutions become more cooperative and less competitive with the board of regents playing a crucial role.

The Murky Future of Higher Education in the United States

Concluding Remarks

As the above chapters indicate, a number of salient issues will have a significant effect on higher education for the foreseeable future. Critical among these are:

1. Transformation from a Collegial to a Corporate Model

Colleges and universities have been transformed as if by stealth and without serious national debate from a collegial structure to a corporate one. Faculty in schools of education where such issues should have primacy are inexplicably silent and other faculty have not been mobilized to examine the ramifications. Of special importance is the effect of corporatization on faculty's role in shared governance. What are the implications of this change long-term? Of relevance are the issues of tenure and promotion, academic standards, entrepreneurship, and unionization.

2. Leadership and the Financial Imperative

Related to the corporatization of colleges and universities is the type of academic leader selected for senior positions. No longer are college presidents chosen for their academic accomplishments, their vision for the future, importance of standards, and their effectiveness in relating to faculty, staff, students, and other institutional constituencies. Rather they are selected primarily for their prowess as fundraisers and skills in public relations. They view their roles like corporate CEOs, deserving of all the perquisites and benefits of the position. Since the types of

Failed Grade

academic leaders of a previous era are rarely found, how will this change affect the future of higher education?

3. Access and Exploding Tuition Costs

Probably one of the more critical issues is the fact that tuition costs have been rising at double-digit rates for the past two decades—at least double the national inflation rate. Highly qualified poor and middle-class students are finding the land-grant concept of education and access a mirage. Those with a responsibility to curb this development are not responding and finger pointing has begun. What will the composition of the student body be, if current trends continue?

4. Students and Their Expectations

Because of financial pressures, more students must work to pay for their education. One consequence is that students increasingly view college as a part-time activity. Their objective is to obtain a degree as rapidly as possible in order to secure a high-paying job. They view themselves as "customers," deserving of a degree as long as they can pay for it and high academic standards are an unaccepted impediment. A crucial question is how will such an environment affect the quality of tomorrow's graduates? And will American higher education continue to be a beacon for international students who have been an important segment of the student population?

The Murky Future of Higher Education in the United States

5. Challenges and the Future

In the aftermath of the terrorist attack of September 11, 2001, the collapse of certain major corporations, and the Iraq War of 2003, the vision and ingenuity of academic leaders will be sorely challenged in finding creative ways to fund public and private institutions. The former are especially vulnerable as the reduction in state support is vitiating the land-grant concept. Already fewer international students are coming here for chemistry graduate programs,[21] and such changes have affected other disciplines as fewer visas are being granted. The full effect of the issues and problems cited above and in the previous chapters may not be manifest for several decades or more. Yet, they will have a profound effect on the type of faculty and administrators recruited, the learning environment, and student expectations. As Hegel, the 19th century German philosopher, said, "Hell is truth seen too late." These concerns have been my primary reason for writing this book. I hope it will stimulate wider discussion of these critical issues so important for the future of higher education in America.

Endnotes

Chapter 1. The Not-So-Recent Past

1. Henry D. Smyth, *Atomic Energy for Military Purposes.* Princeton: Princeton University Press, 1945.
2. Robert S. Norris, *Racing for the Bomb—General Leslie R. Groves, The Manhattan Project's Indispensable Man.* Hanover, N.H.: Steerforth Press, 2002.
3. "History of the GI Bill." University of Central Florida—Office of Veterans' Affairs, 2002.
4. Russell Jacoby, *Dogmatic Wisdom—How the Culture Wars Divert Education and Distract America.* New York: Doubleday, 1994, p.5.

Failed Grade

Chapter 2. The New Financial Imperative

1. Eric Gould, *The University in a Corporate Culture.* New Haven, Conn.: Yale University Press, 2003, p.29.
2. Ronald G. Corwin, *Education in Crisis: A Sociological Analysis of Schools and Universities in Transition.* New York: John Wiley & Sons, Inc., 1974, p.59.
3. Sheila Slaughter and Larry L. Leslie, *Academic Capitalism—Politics, Policies, and the Entrepreneurial University.* Baltimore: Johns Hopkins University Press, 1999.
4. Stanley Aronowitz, *The Knowledge Factory: Dismantling the Corporate University and Creating True Higher Learning.* Boston: Beacon Press, 2000.
5. Randy Martin, *Chalk Lines: The Politics of Work in the Managed University.* Durham: Duke University Press, 1999.
6. Geoffry D. White, Flannery C. Hauk, Geoffrey W. White, eds., , *Campus, Inc.: Corporate Power in the Ivory Tower.* Amherst, NY: Prometheus Books, 2001.
7. "Selling Out? Corporations on Campus." *ACADEME—* Bulletin of the American Association of University Professors. Volume 87, Number 5, September-October 2001.
8. James J. Duderstadt, *Intercollegiate Athletics and the American University: A University President's Perspective.* Ann Arbor: University of Michigan Press, 2000, pp. 73-76.
9. Ibid., p.222.

Endnotes

10. Murray Sperber, *Beer and Circus—How Big-Time College Sports Is Crippling Undergraduate Education.* New York: Henry Holt and Company, 2000.
11. James L. Shulman and William G. Bowen, *The Game of Life—College Sports and Educational Values.* Princeton: Princeton University Press, 2001.
12. Robert M. Rosenzweig, *The Political University—Policy, Politics, and Presidential Leadership in the American Research University.* Baltimore: Johns Hopkins University Press, 2001.
13. Derek Bok, *Universities in the Marketplace—The Commercialization of Higher Education.* Princeton: Princeton University Press, 2003, p.112.
14. Williams C. Symonds and Rich Miller, "Harvard—Larry Summers has an ambitious agenda to remake the nation's leading university. Can he do it?," *BusinessWeek*, February 18, 2002, p. 72.

Chapter 3. The Organization

1. Ronald G. Corwin, *Education in Crisis: A Sociological Analysis of Schools and Universities in Transition.* New York: John Wiley & Sons, Inc., 1974, p. 64.
2. Nancy P. Goldschmidt and James H. Finkelstein, "Academics on Board—University Presidents as Corporate Directors." *Academe*, September-October, 2001, pp. 22-27.
3. Robert C. and Jon Solomon, *Up the University—Recreating Higher Education in America.* Reading MA : Addison-Wesley, 1993, p. 33.

Failed Grade

4. Eyal Press and Jennifer Washburn, "The Kept University." *The Atlantic Monthly*, March 2000, pp. 39-54.
5. Henry Rosovsky, *"The University: An Owner's Manual.* New York: W.W. Norton, 1990, p. 255. "Cultivate the art of asking for money; your career may depend on the results."
6. Clara M. Lovett, "The dumbing down of college presidents." *The Chronicle of Higher Education*, April 5, 2002, B20.
7. David Bercuson, Robert Bothwell, and J. L. Granatstein, *Petrified Campus—The Crisis in Canada's Universities*. Toronto: Random House Canada, 1997, p.5. "The major problems (with the erosion of quality) were all connected to universities having become instruments of public policy rather than institutions of learning."
8. Derek Bok, *Universities in the Marketplace---The Commercialization of Higher Education*. Princeton: Princeton University Press, 2003, p.191.

Chapter 4. Boards of Trustees

1. Kate Zernike, "At Auburn, a challenge to a trustee's reign." *The New York Times*, July 26, 2002, A12.
2. Julianne Basinger and Seth Perry, "Private funds drive up pay of public-university presidents." *The Chronicle of Higher Education*, August 30, 2002, pp. 6-11.
3. "Chema named Hiram College president," *The Columbus Dispatch,* February 3, 2004.

Endnotes

Chapter 5. Boards of Regents or State Boards of Higher Education

1. Donald E. Heller, ed., *The States and Public Higher Education Policy*. Baltimore: Johns Hopkins University Press, 2001.
2. Albert A. Belmonte, private communication.
3. James Martin, James E. Samels, and Associates, *Merging Colleges for Mutual Growth—A New Strategy for Academic Managers*. Baltimore: Johns Hopkins University Press, 2000.
4. Alice Thomas, "Grads require a boost in college—38% of Ohioans took remedial classes at state public schools," *The Columbus Dispatch*, July 12, 2002.

Chapter 6. Faculty and Tenure Matters

1. Annette Kolodny, *Failing the Future—A Dean Looks at Higher Education in the Twenty-first Century*." Durham: Duke University Press, 1998, p.60. "After all, when tenure works properly, a junior faculty member is subjected to fair and vigorous review over a five-to-seven year period. At a research university (and at most colleges and universities), the faculty member must demonstrate excellence in both teaching and research—or creative work—in order to be granted tenure."
2. Frank H. T. Rhodes, *The Creation of the Future—The Role of the American University*. Ithaca: Cornell University Press, 2001, pp. 151-57.

Failed Grade

3. James F. Carlin, "To Reduce Tuition." In letter to the editor, *The New York Times*, May 12, 2002.
4. David Bercuson, Robert Bothwell, and J. L. Granatstein, *Petrified Campus—The Crisis in Canada's Universities.* Toronto: Random House Canada, 1997, p.152. "The only answer, therefore, is limited-term, renewable contracts. The good faculty—the competent researchers and the effective teachers—will have no trouble continuing their careers successfully under this regime. With luck and some administrative courage, the deadwood, no longer protected by job-security tenure, will be pruned at last."
5. Annette Kolodny, *Failing the Future—A Dean Looks at Higher Education in the Twenty-first Century.* Durham: Duke University Press, 1998, pp. 53-67.
6. Henry Rosovsky, *The University: An Owner's Manual.* New York: W.W. Norton, 1990, pp. 179-80. "Let me now try to state the affirmative case for tenure as one of the necessary virtues of academic life. The first habitual line of defense is tenure as the principal guarantor of academic freedom."
7. Zachary Karabell, *What's College For? The Struggle to Define American Higher Education.* New York: Basic Books, 1998, p. 139. "Defenders of tenure are quick to point out that even granting the problems, the alternatives are worse. They may be right."
8. Ellen Willis, "Why professors turn to organized labor," *The New York Times*, May 28, 2001.
9. Henry Rosovsky, *The University: An Owner's Manual.* New York: W.W. Norton, 1990, p.261.

Endnotes

10. Frank H. T. Rhodes, *The Creation of the Future—The Role of the American University.* Ithaca: Cornell University Press, 2001, p. 233.

Chapter 7. Students and Their Expectations

1. Zachary Karabell, *What's College For? The Struggle to Define American Higher Education.* New York: Basic Books, 1998, pp. vii-viii. "Today, the 'value of an education' is calculated in a more straightforward way: in terms of lifetime dollars and cents potentially to be earned. Indeed, working- and middle-class parents are now regularly spending or borrowing $50,000 to $100,000 per child to give their children the benefits of a college education because they know that without the degree their child's life chances will be severely restricted. And there is little disagreement on this point. That college is the single most important factor in getting launched in a career is no longer challenged by anyone, at least not in the U.S."
2. Frank H. T. Rhodes, *The Creation of the Future—The Role of the American University.* Ithaca: Cornell University Press, 2001, p. 64-65.
3. David D. Perlmutter, "Going to college? Here's how to fail," *The Columbus Dispatch*, August 3, 2002.
4. Zachary Karabell, *What's College For? The Struggle to Define American Higher Education.* New York: Basic Books, 1998, pp. 234-35.
5. Peter F. Drucker, *The Effective Executive.* New York: Harper & Row, 1967, pp. 60-61.

Failed Grade

6. Quoted by Aruna Jagtiani, "Ford lends support to Ohio State," *Ohio State Lantern*, July 14, 1994, p.1.
7. Williams C. Symonds and Rich Miller, "Harvard and Beyond," *BusinessWeek*, February 18, 2002, pp. 73-78.

Chapter 8. Education versus Indoctrination—How Social and Political Agendas Discourage Independent Thinking

1. Zachary Karabell, *What's College For? The Struggle to Define American Higher Education*. New York: Basic Books, 1998, p.13.
2. Ibid., p.6.
3. Ibid., p. x.
4. Robert C. and Jon Solomon, *Up the University—Recreating Higher Education in America*. Reading MA: Addison-Wesley, 1993, p.6.
5. Ibid., p.159.
6. David Bromwich, *Politics by Other Means—Higher Education and Group Thinking*. New Haven: Yale University Press, 1992, pp. 3-52.
7. Steven Conn, Associate Professor of History, The Ohio State University, "Hard sell: The University as a product," *The Columbus Dispatch*, July 21, 2001.
8. Frank H. T. Rhodes, *The Creation of the Future—The Role of the American University*. Ithaca: Cornell University Press, 2001, pp. 64-65.

Endnotes

Chapter 9. The Problem with the Leadership-Selection Process

1. Robert C. and Jon Solomon, *Up the University—Recreating Higher Education in America*. Reading MA: Addison-Wesley, 1993, p.36.
2. Clara M. Lovett, "The dumbing down of college presidents," *The Chronicle of Higher Education*, April 5, 2002, B20.
3. Annette Kolodny, *Failing the Future—A Dean Looks at Higher Education in the Twenty-first Century*. Durham: Duke University Press, 1998, p.30. "Search committees for administrators might emphasize the individual who can build community without silencing debate or disagreement, the individual who is comfortable with diversity and inclusivity."

Chapter 10. Attributes for Administrative Success and Failure

1. Henry Mintzberg, *The Nature of Managerial Work*. Englewood Cliffs, NJ: Prentice Hall, 1986.
2. Frank H. T. Rhodes, *The Creation of the Future—The Role of the American University*. Ithaca: Cornell University Press, 2001, pp. 222-28.
3. Niccolo Machiavelli, *The Prince*, translated and edited by Angelo M. Codevilla, commentary by William B. Allen, Hadley Arkes, and Carnes Lord. New Haven: Yale University Press, 1997, p.87.

Failed Grade

4. Allan Bloom , *The Closing of the American Mind: How Higher Education Has Failed Democracy and Impoverished the Souls of Today's Students.* New York: Simon & Schuster, 1986, p.42. Though Dr. Bloom was not discussing administrators, his comment applies very aptly. "True openness means closedness to all the charms that make us comfortable with the present."
5. Robert C. and Jon Solomon, *Up the University— Recreating Higher Education in America.* Reading MA: Addison-Wesley, 1993, p. 33. "Administrators come to think of themselves as the university just as corporate management has come to think of itself as the corporation".

Chapter 11. First Days on the Job

1. Ashley Montagu, *The Natural Superiority of Women.* Walnut Creek CA: AltaMira Press, 1999, p.58. "These difficulties are all problems in human relations and until they are solved, human beings will in large numbers continue to behave unintelligently and ineffectually."

Chapter 12. Administrative Sensitivity

1. A Nobel Prize colleague in one of the Ivy League schools told me he had assumed the chair of his department. He felt a responsibility to the department and his colleagues. After a three-year stint, he returned to the faculty. He had been very successful during that time in increasing the department's endowment.

Endnotes

Chapter 13. Ethics and the Administrator

1. Chester I. Barnard, *The Functions of the Executive.* Cambridge: Harvard University Press, 1968, p. 273.
2. William W. May, ed., *Ethics and Higher Education.* New York: American Council on Education and Macmillan Publishing Co., 1990.
3. Amy Gutmann, "How can universities teach professional ethics?" in *Universities and Their Leadership*, William G. Bowen and Harold T. Shapiro, eds. Princeton, N.J.: Princeton University Press, 1998, p. 166.
4. Allan Bloom , *The Closing of the American Mind: How Higher Education Has Failed Democracy and Impoverished the Souls of Today's Students.* New York: Simon & Schuster, 1986, p. 61.
5. Ibid., p. 59.
6. Chester I. Barnard, *The Functions of the Executive.* Cambridge: Harvard University Press, 1968, p. 293.

Chapter 14. Recruitment, Retention, and Termination of Colleagues and Subordinates

1. Bill Readings, *The University in Ruins.* Cambridge: Harvard University Press, 1996, p. 22. "Generally, we hear a lot of talk from university administrators about excellence, because it has become the unifying principle of the contemporary university."

Failed Grade

2. Frank H. T. Rhodes, *The Creation of the Future—The Role of the American University*. Ithaca, N.Y.: Cornell University Press, 2001, p. 36.
3. Lester A. Mitscher, PhD, private communication.

Chapter 15. Environment Creation, Decision Making, and Problem Solving

1. Peter F. Drucker, *The Effective Executive*. New York: Harper & Row, 1967, p. 113.
2. Ibid., pp. 37-38.

Chapter 16. Maximizing the Contributions of Associates

1. Peter F. Drucker, *The Effective Executive*. New York: Harper & Row, 1967, p.51.
2. Ibid., p. 45.

Chapter 17. Administration Compensation, Financial Decision Making, and Budget Utilization

1. Julianne Basinger and Seth Perry, "Private funds drive up pay of public-university presidents," *The Chronicle of Higher Education*, pp. 6-11, August 30, 2002.
2. David Leonhardt, "The imperial chief executive is suddenly in the cross hairs," *The New York Times*, June 24, 2002, p. 1.
3. William J. Studer, PhD, personal communication.
4. 1970-71 Current Funds Budget, as presented to the president and the board of trustees of The Ohio State

Endnotes

University. Prepared by The Office of University Budgets, June 11, 1970.

5. Alice Thomas, "Grads require a boost in college—38% of Ohioans took remedial classes at state public schools," *The Columbus Dispatch*, July 12, 2002.

6. Robert C. and Jon Solomon, *Up the University— Recreating Higher Education in America*. Reading: Addison-Wesley, 1993, p. 32. "Not only is the university not driven by the 'bottom line' (most good corporations are not either), but the corporate mentality infects the university administration in more insidious ways."

7. Henry Rosovsky, *The University: An Owner's Manual*. New York: W.W. Norton, 1990, pp. 233-34.

Chapter 18. Colleges and Universities as Money-Generating Machines

1. Alice Thomas, "The money machine," *The Columbus Dispatch*, June 2, 2002, p.1.

2. Ibid., Jerry May, former vice president for development at The Ohio State University.

3. Daniel Golden and Charles Forelle, "Colleges feel pinch as endowments shrink," *The Wall Street Journal*, July 19, 2002, p. B1.

4. Current Funds Budget 2001-2002 of The Ohio State University, Prepared by The Office of Resource Planning, August 29, 2001.

Failed Grade

Chapter 19. The Ballooning Costs of Higher Education and Who's Worrying About It

1. Ibbotson Association Inc. and the College Entrance Examination Board—College costs are rising twice as fast as inflation in the last ten years, the cost of a college education has nearly doubled with the escalating costs of tuition, room and board, fees, books and transportation. Costs at private schools today amount to 44 percent of the average middle-class family's income compared with 27 percent in 1980.
2. Jacques Steinberg, "More family income committed to college," *The New York Times*, May 2, 2002.
3. Robert M. Shireman, "Enrolling economic diversity," *The New York Times*, May 4, 2002.
4. Indicator 22. College Costs—Average charges for full-time undergraduate students, by type and control of college: 1959-60 to 1992-93, U.S. Department of Education, National Center for Education Statistics, Digest of Education Statistics, 1993; and Projections of Education Statistics to 1979-80. http://www.ed.gov/pubs/YouthIndicators/indtab22.html .
5. Annette Kolodny, *Failing the Future—A Dean Looks at Higher Education in the Twenty-first Century*. Durham: Duke University Press, 1998, p. 253.
6. James F. Carlin, "To reduce tuition," in letter to the editor, *The New York Times*, May 12, 2002.

Endnotes

7a. 1970-71 Current Funds Budget of The Ohio State University prepared by The Office of University Budgets June 11, 1970.

7b. The Ohio State University Current Funds Budget 1990-91, June 1, 1990.

7c. The Ohio State University Current Funds Budget 2001-2002, Prepared by The Office of Resource Planning, August 29, 2001. Unfortunately, this budget lacked the information available in 7a and 7b.

8. I want to acknowledge the suggestions of Dr. William J. Studer, former Director of the Libraries of The Ohio State University, and the invaluable help of Ms. Bertha Ihnat, Assistant for Manuscripts, at the University Archives at The Ohio State University for the documents she provided me, and the time she spent with me.

9. AFT On Campus, "Fighting bloat in Illinois," December 2002/January 2003.

10. "Academic Plan is Ohio State's rallying cry for greatness," *On Campus*, The Ohio State University/Faculty/Staff/News, Volume 31, Number 22, June 13, 2002.

11. Kathy L. Gray, "College gets more costly as schools push limits," *The Columbus Dispatch*, April 18, 2004.

12. Kathy L. Gray, "OSU tuition hike worries students," *The Columbus Dispatch,* May 8, 2004.

Chapter 20. The Legacy of Faculty and Academic Administrators

Failed Grade

1. Allan Bloom, *The Closing of the American Mind: How Higher Education Has Failed Democracy and Impoverished the Souls of Today's Students.* New York: Simon & Schuster, 1986, p. 22.
2. Lord Krishna, the great Hindu religious leader, in "Bhagwad Gita."

Chapter 21. The Murky Future of Higher Education in the United States

1. Frank H. T. Rhodes, *The Creation of the Future—The Role of the American University.* Ithaca, N.Y.: Cornell University Press, 2001, pp. 229-44.
2. James Duderstadt, *Intercollegiate Athletics and the American University: A University President's Perspective.* Ann Arbor: University of Michigan Press, 2000.
3. James L. Shulman and William G. Bowen, *The Game of Life—College Sports and Educational Values.* Princeton, N.J.: Princeton University Press, 2001.
4. Murray Sperber, *Beer and Circus—How Big-Time College Sports Is Crippling Undergraduate Education.* New York: Henry Holt and Company, 2000.
5. Kate Zernike, "At Auburn, a challenge to a trustee's reign," *The New York Times,* July 26, 2002, A12.
6. William A. Henry III, *In Defense of Elitism.* New York: Doubleday, 1994.
7. James Duderstadt, *Intercollegiate Athletics and the American University: A University President's*

Endnotes

Perspective. Ann Arbor: University of Michigan Press, 2000, pp.208-13.

8. Robert C. and Jon Solomon, *Up the University— Recreating Higher Education in America*. Reading: Addison-Wesley, 1993, p. 287.

9. June Kronholz, "As amount of funding declines, public universities trim state ties," *The Wall Street Journal*, April 18, 2003.

10. Timothy Egan, "States, facing budget shortfalls, cut the major and the mundane," *The New York Times,* April 21, 2003, A1.

11. Sam Dillon, "University plans to double in-state tuition," *The New York Times,* April 5, 2003.

12. Alice Thomas, "Where the money goes," *The Columbus Dispatch*, April 27, 2003, A1.

13. David Leonhardt, "As wealthy fill top colleges, concerns grow over fairness," *The New York Times,* April 22, 2004.

14. Alice Thomas, "Prepaid tuition rates rise by 7%," *The Columbus Dispatch*, May 2, 2003, C1.

15. Mark K. Anderson, "Analysis: Setting the payment standards of online-education", September 29, 2000. http://asia.cnn.com/2000/TECH/computing/09/29/onlin e.ed.pay.idg/.

16. Gerald Graffe, *Beyond the Culture Wars: How Teaching the Conflicts Can Revitalize American Education.* New York: W. W. Norton, 1992, p. 193.

17. Eric Gould, *The University in a Corporate Culture.* New Haven, Conn.: Yale University Press, 2003.

Failed Grade

18. William C. Symonds and Rich Miller, "Harvard—Larry Summers has an ambitious agenda to remake the nation's leading university. Can he do it?" *BusinessWeek,* February 18, 2002, p.72.
19. Joan Lippert, "The commercialization of university medical research," *The P&S Journal*, Spring 1998, Vol. 18, No. 2, Ethics in Medicine. http://cpmcnet.columbia.edu/news/journal/archives/jour_v18no2_0012.html.
20. Lawrence C. Soley, *Leasing the Ivory Tower: The Corporate Takeover of Academia.* New York: South End Press, 1998.
21. V. Gilman and W. G. Schulz, "U.S. schools losing foreign talent," *Chemical & Engineering News*, April 5, 2004, pp. 67-70.

Failed Grade

Index

a

academic-industrial-political complex 36
administrative
      compensation 187, 189, 228, 243
      costs 35, 64, 65, 131, 190, 191, 192, 193
      deferred compensation 188, 189
      sensitivity 112, 117, 119, 135, 136, 138,
175, 225
      vision 39, 112, 172, 250
Affirmative Action 231, 233, 240
Americans with Disabilities Act 10, 191
athletic assistantships 232
austerity 247

b

Barnard, Chester I. 139, 146
Black and Hispanic faculty 240
Bloom, Allan 145, 146, 223
Bok, Derek 19, 27, 41, 187
Bromwich, David 98
budgetary transparency 248
business speak 15

Index

c

career decision/options   79, 80, 81, 237, 238
Chronicle of Higher Education, The   187, 188
Civil Rights Act   10
Clark University   52
College Entrance Examination Board and Ibbotson
 Association Inc.   207
collegial environment   xii, 14, 44 , 77, 118, 127, 164, 189,
 253
Columbia University   42, 44
cooperative education   237
corporate culture/corporatization   xii, xiv, 14, 31, 33, 34,
 43, 44, 46, 75, 93, 139, 144, 157, 167, 173, 174, 178,
 187, 189, 193, 229, 244, 253
Corwin, Ronald   14, 33
cost containment/control   17, 248
Cox, Harvey   124

d

distance learning   101, 236, 246
diversity   97, 98, 190, 209, 233, 235, 239, 240,
downsizing & restructuring   17, 62, 63, 67, 234
Drucker, Peter F.   89, 182, 183
Duderstadt, James   18, 230

e

Einstein, Albert   162

277

Failed Grade

elitism 231
endowment 20, 34, 39, 186, 204, 205, 218, 219
entrepreneurship xiv, 16, 20, 130, 142, 153, 253
environment creation 167, 168, 169, 171, 177, 179, 209
Equal Employment Opportunity Act 10
ethical environment/principles 27, 120, 140, 142, 143, 144, 146, 147, 251

f

faculty
     consulting 26
     development 4, 129
     early retirement 70, 175
     governance 46, 78, 240, 241, 242
financial imperative 13, 16, 26, 30, 31, 32, 139, 201
Folkman, Judah 24
fundraising 21, 24, 32, 34, 35, 38, 39, 45, 188, 200, 201, 202, 203, 205, 214, 219, 243, 249, 253

g

G.I. Bill 7
Gee, E. Gordon 89
Gould, Eric 13, 238
grade inflation 28, 29, 30
graduation rates 20, 29, 30, 31
Gutmann, Amy 139

h

Index

Hampden School of Pharmacy   59
Hegel, G. W. F.   255
Hillel, Rabbi   140
Hippocratic Oath   186
Hiram College   55
Hunt, Albert R.   231
Huxley, Thomas   88

i

imperial presidency   188
institutional governance   xiv, 55, 78
intellectual property   37
inter- institutional collaboration   251, 252

k

Karabell, Zachary   95, 96
King, Martin Luther Jr.   235
Kolodny, Annette   209
Krishna, Lord   227

l

Laybourne, Geraldine   105
legacy admissions   2
Leonhardt, David   235
leveraging   197
litigious environment   111, 125, 155, 191, 211, 226, 233

279

Failed Grade

long-range planning   173, 174

m

Machiavelli, Niccolo   121
managerial accounting   196
Manhattan Project -- atomic bomb   5, 8
Mencken, H. L.   124
Mintzberg, Henry   117
multicultural society   164, 235

n

National Defense Education Act   8

o

Occupational Safety and Health Authority (OSHA)   191
Ohio State University, The 19, 21, 74, 214, 220
online universities   16, 101
overhead monies   23, 244

p

Perlmutter, David D   85
plagiarizing   158
profit center   15, 17, 153, 193, 243
publish or perish   23

r

Index

remedial education   3, 66, 95, 190
Rhodes, Frank H. T.   78, 118, 150
Rosovsky, Henry   73, 77, 194
Russell, Bertrand   97, 100

s

salary-recovery plan   25, 201
search firms   110, 111
September 11, 2001   11, 255
shared governance   15, 42, 242, 243, 253
Shaw, George Bernard   134
Shawnee State University   60, 61
Solomon, Robert C. and Jon   34, 35, 96, 107, 235
South Carolina   64
Sputnik   8
start-up costs   22
Stowe, C. E.   136
students
         consumer mentality   83, 89, 90, 97, 238, 239, 254
         dumbing down   95
         peer pressure   234
         social promotion   89, 91
Summers, Lawrence H.   28, 239

t

technology   245, 246, 247
term appointments   42, 73, 76

Failed Grade

Title IX of the Higher Education Act   232
title-inflation   186
Trinity College   15, 16
Truman, Harry   163, 184
Twain, Mark   85

u,v,w

unfunded mandates   65, 190, 213
unionization   76, 77, 242, 253
Vietnam War   10, 11, 85, 99
White, Andrew D.   84, 103

Acknowledgements

The ideas for this book have been percolating in my mind for many years. Thanks to the help and encouragement of many colleagues and friends, whose opinions I value, it became a reality.

I am especially indebted to two individuals, Professor Emeritus Simon Dinitz for his continual encouragement and our many discussions throughout my entire effort and his writing an endorsement on my behalf; and to former Provost and Professor Emeritus Albert Kuhn for his editing advice, willingness to write the Foreword, and his constructive criticism. Both of them were enormously helpful in focusing me on my primary reason for writing this book.

And, I especially want to thank my wife, Barbara, for her great forbearance, as I spent countless hours on the computer preparing one version after another and also for her critical suggestions and support of the final title. I wish to thank my three children, Madeleine Carolan, Paul Soloway and Renee Spiegler, and their spouses, Chris, Debbie and Paul and my brother, Sidney and his wife, Rhoda, for their

Failed Grade

encouragement and great interest throughout my effort. All have made a crucial difference.

I want to acknowledge as well Michael Pastore of Zorba Press who was very supportive and helped me concentrate on what needed to be done in the initial phases to get this manuscript in its current form.

I wish to thank as well Professor Raymond Doskotch, Ms. Laura Zakin, and Deacon Anthony Bonacci for their comments on earlier versions of this manuscript and portions thereof. And I also want to thank Drs. Dev Pathak and Eve Levin for their endorsements; Drs. Rolf Barth, my very close research colleague and great friend who encouraged the preparation of an index; John Neumeyer, long time colleague and very dear friend; Michael Gerald; Carter Olson; Popat Patil; Robert Curley; Dennis McKay; Henry Hunker; Mervin Muller; Philip Smith; George Smith; William Studer; Earl Murphy; Gideon Fraenkel; Samuel Osipow; Roy Koenigsknecht; James Bishop; Victor and Ann Warner; Dennis Worthen; David Rigney; Jack Zakin; Allan Burkman; Norman Uretsky; Larry Robertson; Arnold Goldstein who was responsible for suggesting the book's title; Ms. Adrienne Chafetz; Ms. Angela Staubus; and Dean Emeritus Lloyd Parks for their encouragement, and in some instances, useful discussions and suggestions. I want to thank as well Jack Fowble for his interest and computer help and Marty Marlatt for creating the Index and putting the book in its final form. That assistance has been invaluable.

I am also indebted to Lee Nunn of The American Book Company for his acceptance of this manuscript and to

Acknowledgements

Editors Lou Belcher, Allan Macpherson, Todd Hansen, Jeffrey Townsend, and Ms. Erin Paisan, all of whom played very significant roles in its editing and to Jana Rade, Director of Design for the book's cover.

About the Author

Dr. Soloway graduated from the Worcester Polytechnic Institute with a BS in Chemistry and from the University of Rochester with a PhD in Organic Chemistry. He was a post-doctoral Fellow of the National Cancer Institute at Sloan-Kettering Institute for Cancer Research and a research chemist at Eastman Kodak. He worked for ten years as a research chemist in the Department of Neurosurgery at the Massachusetts General Hospital, part of the teaching facilities of the Harvard Medical School. His academic career began as Associate Professor in the College of Pharmacy at Northeastern University. During eleven years there, he became Professor, Chair of the Department of Medicinal Chemistry and Pharmacology, and Dean of the College of Pharmacy and Allied Health Professions. He taught professional and graduate courses, conducted research sponsored by the National Cancer Institute and the Department of Energy, and educated graduate students, postdoctoral fellows, and research associates.

Failed Grade

In 1977, he was recruited by The Ohio State University for the position of Dean of the College of Pharmacy and Professor of Medicinal Chemistry, serving as dean for eleven years. After retiring as dean, he returned to the faculty for ten more years before retiring in 1998 as Kimberly Professor.

Dr. Soloway authored more than two hundred scientific publications in peer-reviewed journals, generated tens of millions of dollars in grants from government agencies to support his research, and was a founder and president of the International Society for Neutron Capture Therapy, dedicated to finding an experimental radiation method for treating malignant brain tumors. He is Fellow of the American Association for the Advancement of Science and Fellow of the Association of Pharmaceutical Scientists. He served as a consultant to the Department of Energy, the National Cancer Institute, the Hebrew University in evaluating their School of Pharmacy, and international agencies. He was a visiting scientist at Brookhaven National Laboratory, the Paul Scherrer Institute in Switzerland, and the Australian Nuclear Science and Technology Organization. He is listed in *Who's Who in American Men and Women in Science* and is Dean and Professor Emeritus at The Ohio State University.

He is married to Barbara (Berkowicz) Soloway and they have three children and six grandchildren. He was President of the Torch Club of Columbus 2004-2005.